ELECTED THROUGH
TERROR

The Rajneesh through the eyes of a local sheriff

By Art Labrousse

Published by Between the Presses, LLC.

This book is an original publication of Between the Presses. All rights reserved.

First Printing, September 2016

ISBN-13: 978-1535070065

ISBN-10: 1535070064

Publisher's Note

All events portrayed in this book occurred in Wasco County, Oregon between 1981 and 1985, unless otherwise noted. Events described are as the author remembers them. Names, places, and incidents are a matter of public record. Any inaccuracy is unintentional.

Dedication

This book is dedicated to the citizens, commissioners and the Planning Office of Wasco County. You lived through and stood tall during the terrorism by the Rajneesh leaders.

And to my wife and children. You helped me and stood by me in these difficult times.

Contents

FOREWORD

Over seven hundred and fifty people were poisoned in one day. Arson, immigration fraud, attempted murder, election fraud, and many other crimes committed by the leadership. As County Sheriff, it was my job was to deal with the situation. Through the years, I have been asked by many to write about my experiences with the Rajneesh. I had many challenging things on my plate that first year. The main one, of course, being the Rajneesh, but it was not the only issue I considered Priority One.

Not every Rajneesh was a criminal. County citizens, the majority of the followers, and others attached to the compound had nothing to do with the terrorism. Even members of the commune were targeted. All they wanted to do was be near the Bhagwan Shree Rajneesh. They wanted to be with him. Listen to him. Worship him. He was their god. However, those that were involved created a great deal of mayhem.

Hiding behind the cloak of religion, these people got away with terrorist acts for several years. The State refused to investigate for two main reasons. First, the Rajneesh used the media to bully any who opposed their "freedom of religious expression," even when their religion called for human suffering of anyone not part of the sect. Second, the Rajneesh leaders used the weapon of yelling "bigot" against any and all who opposed their actions. Non-compliant county officials and other citizens were labeled "rednecks" or accused of overreacting. And not just by the Rajneesh, but by people who lived elsewhere and didn't understand what was happening. News media didn't do anything to counteract that; many of them believed Wasco County citizens were bigots.

These people had good reason to be concerned about the Rajneesh's activities. They committed the first documented germ warfare against American citizens by poisoning salad bars, water sources, and other public spaces. Hundreds of people became ill. Some are still suffering from the effects of that poisoning today, both physically and mentally. Businesses were destroyed. The Rajneesh also developed and tried other tactics to poison or physically attack citizens across all of Oregon, going as far as growing biological weapons on their compound.

In the end, the truth won out. The State Attorney General began his investigation and lawsuits against the cities early in their occupation, but the rest of the State of Oregon got their eyes opened up, and some of the followers were prosecuted. Sadly, several escaped into countries with no extradition agreements.

How much the leader, Rajneesh himself, knew about the criminal activity remains unclear. Nor can the exact financial and emotional cost of the terrorism in his name be calculated. However, tens of thousands of hours were spent investigating violations and defending the laws of Wasco County and the State of Oregon. Time, of course, was money. Money that was needed in other areas.

Wasco was one of the larger counties in Oregon with one of the smallest populations per capita. The damage to its small towns was beyond measure. As a concerned citizen of the county, I stepped up to fight this injustice by running for county sheriff. Upon winning, my goal became to protect and serve the people. This book reflects those memories as well as the other challenges I faced that divided my attention that first year in office.

CHAPTER 1

Rajneesh followers called themselves Sannyasins. The name did not stick outside their inner circles. Everyone else called them the Rajneesh. Even to this day one would be hard pressed to find them called anything else.

Though the age range ran from late teens to the elderly, the leaders were in their 30's and 40's. They were successful professionals in their fields. The Bhagwan Rajneesh called himself the spiritual guru to the rich.

My opinion is that while many of their fellow collegians were whooping it up in the 1960's and 1970's with drugs and "free love," these men and women studied hard and strove to be the best in their field. They became successful. Their high motivation brought them wealth, but little fulfillment.

They all reached a plateau in their lives where the gathering of material wealth was no longer rewarding. Their spiritual condition haunted them. They went in search of something that would lift them up and make them feel good about themselves: a higher being that would relate to them, giving them spiritual relief. They found the Bhagwan Shree Rajneesh. Buying into his teachings, many gave all their worldly possessions to honor him.

They clambered to be near him, study with him, and live life in his community. As their numbers grew so did their need to find a place. Fed up with the Rajneesh's intimidation tactics, the Indian government refused to give into the demands of the group. The Rajneesh leadership turned to America: land of the free and home of the brave. They thought they could get away with anything here.

The Bhagwan Rajneesh took a vow of silence until his followers found a permanent home in America. Ma Anand Sheela became his voice for quite some time. She was the undisputed leader and spokesperson of the group, conferring and conspiring with the Bhagwan Rajneesh daily.

It was Sheela who searched for the property where they could setup. In the process, she came to the Muddy Ranch in the southeast corner of Wasco County. The land stretched approximately sixty-four thousand acres, one hundred square miles. Plus there was access to thousands of the Bureau of Land Management acreage for cattle grazing.

Sagebrush, Juniper trees, and rock formations made up the bulk of the property. While there was some good soil between the hills, most of the acreage was suitable for cattle and not much else. It took several acres of this kind of land to support one cow. The winters were harsh, and the summers were hot. Lack of water is another big issue that hampers planting and limits what and when things can be grown.

The ranch was isolated from the rest of the county by dirt roads and deep canyons. While a county road went through the center of the property, it was primarily used only by those that were at the ranch or had dealings there. The Dalles, Wasco County's county seat, was located over eighty miles away and, due to the types of roads, it took anywhere upwards of three hours depending on weather to get there.

Sheela decided that the Muddy Ranch was ideal. The isolated location and large plot of land met everything the group looked for. She proceeded to purchase the property without meeting a single neighbor. In 1981 the Rajneesh moved in. They began working on the ranch, reshaping it for their intended purposes.

The nearest community was Antelope, twenty miles away. Antelope was an incorporated city of about twenty-six people, give or take. It had a schoolhouse, a community gathering point that used to be a church, a small general store with gas pumps, and a post office. The county road department also had a shed and equipment placed on the edge of town as a base of operations to work on the roads.

At the turn of the twentieth century, it was a thriving community with hundreds of people and one of the leading sheep processing points in Oregon. But it declined into a community made up of retired people and a few that worked in Madras, a town of about two thousand people twenty-six miles away.

Some things were obvious to me. As I go through this period in my writings, I think I have garnered a little more insight into the mind of the leaders. The Rajneesh accused the local people of being prejudiced towards them because of their religion. While the locals didn't understand the Rajneesh faith, most of them didn't care. Faith was a private thing they lived out through their lives, not a soap box for getting their own way.

The Rajneesh had a very low opinion of the local citizens, shown by their condescending attitudes and actions. The Rajneesh leaders were educated and from a background of privilege. These people bought Rolls Royces by the dozen and traveled in and out of the valley on private planes. One could tell they felt the local citizens were uneducated, unsophisticated and fools. The commune leadership used the media to maximize this image. They took over the local school. They installed their own teachers, naming the old teachers "stupid." It was just the beginning.

Bhagwan was a religious guru and felt entitled to be praised and given special privileges. The excessive wealth bestowed on him by his followers did nothing to discourage that feeling. Sheela, the second in command, came from a wealthy family in India. As we know, India has a caste system, and Sheela's status was at the top.

While America doesn't have a caste system, there were those that believe we have a class system. That was right to a point. Those at the top often felt they were more important than those below them.

However, the farther west you came, the less importance class and money became. More emphasis was placed on how hard you work.

The people that owned the kind of property Sheela was looking for had grown up working side by side with their employees. They were not afraid to get their hands dirty. This size and type of property denoted cattle or sheep. Not hands-clean living. The neighbors of these people were of the same cloth.

The Rajneesh mistook Eastern Oregon hospitality, and a laid back, relaxed lifestyle, for lazy and uneducated. In short, they considered the locals to be country bumpkins they could manipulate. They had little regard for their worth and could care less if they exploited what they thought were backward people who were beneath them.

The residents of Wasco County were grounded people with common sense and a strong sense of right and wrong. They were not uneducated. They were not fools. They were very independent, as would be expected from the stock of the pioneers. They were honest and law abiding and not likely to kowtow to anyone. They were straightforward in the way they dealt with people and were suspicious of those that weren't. They dealt with each other by a nod and handshake and an understanding that each would uphold the verbal contract.

The leaders of the Rajneesh had come from a different environment. They were upset that they didn't get the deference and respect that they were used to getting elsewhere. In their minds, they deserved it because of who they were. They felt they were worthy of high esteem. They thought that their methods would overcome the old ways of the locals and thought their "superior intelligence" would overcome anything the locals could come up with.

Sheela found the Muddy Ranch and, as they drove down, concluded this was where they should go. She spent less than a day on the property. I don't even know if she visited the town of Antelope that first trip. She went into the sale blind to the locals, their ways, and the law of the land. Her confidence was that misplaced.

She was so focused on getting isolated acreage she didn't check to see what the laws were concerning that property. I seriously doubt that she confided in the realtor as to what she wanted to do with the place, or she would have been told no. Her dishonesty and deceit kept her from looking elsewhere and was the start of a four and a half year reign of terror for Wasco County.

In the beginning, the leaders tried to assure the local citizens that all they wanted to do was farm. K.D, aka Krishna Diva, aka David Knapp, was a thorn in the side of Wasco County from the very beginning. Soon after the ranch was purchased, he and a couple of others sat down, wearing non-Rajneesh attire (they always wore bright red and orange clothes, the color of the sunset, and always wore a mala with Rajneesh's picture on it), with the county planner and told him about all the great agriculture ideas they had. They remained careful to not mention the new city they wanted to form. Their stated intent was to bring Rajneesh and a small number of followers to the ranch for agricultural purposes.

Later they paraded the media around, showing off their new "farming techniques." The media became one of their intimidation tactics. They built a dam without permits or checking with local environmental agencies, destroying local wildlife reserves. The backup of water also changed the land's water table, detrimentally affecting the farmers that called this area home.

K.D. left out their primary plan to build a college and other programs dedicated to the Rajneesh and his teachings. They would go as far as to have two sets of plans: one for the county and a real one for their builders. They were deceitful as they voiced their desire to have a farming cooperative with less than two hundred people. They knew full well that more than a thousand people were planning on moving in those first few months, not to mention the thousands that were signed up to visit on their holidays.

In short, they lied.

When they went beyond the laws and were caught in it, they became aggressive. They did whatever they could to make the lives

5

of Wasco County Citizens and their elected officials miserable. They moved in and started building. And it wasn't just structures to house agricultural activity.

They focused on building with only a slight nod to farming. Somehow they thought the local population wouldn't notice, or they could bluff, bribe or even intimidate them. K.D. was one of the ringleaders and seemed to take great joy in his role in the disruption.

For the non-agricultural buildings, they needed permits from the County and had to show why they should be allowed in this area where the zoning was strictly agriculture. They didn't like being told they couldn't build, and they didn't like being told that the process of making those decisions takes time, as well as any appeals they might have to go through.

The Rajneesh couldn't get a meeting facility through the planning process. It was not allowed, so they built a "greenhouse." They didn't need a permit for the building because it was intended for agriculture use.

However, much to their "surprise and consternation," they realized AFTER building it that it was the wrong design and couldn't be used as a "greenhouse." They didn't want to destroy the building; after all, they had spent a lot of money and time in building it. So they decided to keep it up and make it into a meeting hall.

One look at the setting and the way it was designed showed that they deliberately lied.

The building was covered with normal roofing materials. While there were plenty of glass doors on the south side, the wall was filled with them, it was insufficient to allow significant light to help grow plants.

But the real reveal is the way they built a floor-to-ceiling large window on the north side, away from the sun. It was perfectly placed to frame the beautiful rock formations of the area, and the view included the John Day River.

The view really was breathtaking, but the building was not designed to be a "greenhouse." It was designed to be a meeting facility for the commune from the onset.

The "greenhouse" was one of the many buildings that were in contention and going through appeals.

The Rajneesh had been warned by the judge in the first step for the appeal process, which he ruled in favor of the county, that all the work they had been doing could very well be torn down and suggested they wait until the appeal process had been completed before they built anything more.

As with everything else, the Rajneesh "knew better" and continued their trampling of state laws into the ground.

It was said that they figured no one would actually make them remove the buildings after they had been built. There would be so many of them and years would go by, so they may be able to do other things to make them "legal." They felt controlling the County Commission and therefore the County Planning Office would be a reality in a matter of a few short years. Long before the appeal process ended. They could then take it back to the county level and have them approved.

The "greenhouse" and other buildings became a bone of contention and the start of the animosity by the members of the sect towards the county government and the citizens. They wanted what they wanted. What were these country bumpkins to do against a growing population of over two thousand? So despite the permits not being granted, they built businesses and other buildings to support the increasing population.

While some Rajneesh were Americans, they came from larger cities and didn't understand the nuances of ranch life in Eastern Oregon's rural area. They knew the local citizens would be in culture shock over the sect's methods and lifestyle, and they thought they would take advantage of their naiveté. However, they also had a culture shock coming.

On election night in November 1982, I stopped into the Wasco County Courthouse while on patrol. I wanted to see who had won. I saw Bill had been elected to county judge, among others. I talked to several people then, while looking for another person, found Bill in one of the courtrooms surrounded by friends. I had never met him, but knew several of the people in the room and started talking.

Bill was in his sixties, white-haired and a bit stooped. He grew up in Wasco County, outside the small community of Dufur. He was a well-respected wheat rancher. As I shook hands with him, I thought, "This man is so frail. Can he take what the Rajneesh were dealing out?"

During the next two years, I didn't have contact with Bill. He was in the news because of his position, but he was the County Judge, and I was a City Police Officer. Same town, different planets. My contact with the county was with the sheriff's deputies or the district attorney and court system.

From what I could read in the papers and what I heard around town, Bill was holding his own. The Rajneesh hammered him every chance they got. Commissioners were on their hit list. But, as I was wrong in my first assessment, so too were the Rajneesh. Bill was a "tough old bird" from pioneer stock. He was also one of the most humble men I have ever met. After I had been elected, I learned first-hand why Bill was so respected.

The Rajneesh knew they had a lot of people in their organization that were well educated and could be malicious in getting their way. If someone was outspoken about the Rajneesh and their activities, they could expect "presents." Several received boxes of animal feces delivered in the mail.

At least one family received a box of candy. They thought it was from a friend. It wasn't. They found it tainted with a foreign substance and discarded it.

It was not unusual for citizens to go to the mailbox and find that someone had signed them up for pornographic literature. It could not be proven that these packages and mailers came from the Rajneesh.

The thing was, no citizens in the towns had experienced such "presents" before their arrival. The correlation was obvious.

The Rajneesh were well organized (or so they thought) and dedicated to Bhagwan, obeying his every directive as given through his spokesperson, Sheela.

Many were used to bribing officials to get preferential treatment. They soon found out that the elected officials and the County Planning Director would not accept bribes. The County Commissioners were not career politicians. They were men who were active in the community. They had businesses or ranches, and that was how they made their living. They were close to the people they served and took the responsibility of that service serious.

One example was when the Rajneesh purchased some cattle from a county judge (not Bill) while the County Court was in deliberation on whether or not to allow them to have a city on the ranch. I know many people thought the judge had been bribed. That was what the Rajneesh intended. I know this man, and I don't believe it for a minute.

He was a rancher, selling cattle. That was what he did for a living. He did make a mistake selling to them during that time, but there was no doubt in my mind that, while it looked questionable, making that sale had no impact on his decision as a commissioner. He upheld the law as he saw it and did not give the Rajneesh the preferred treatment they expected from a bribed official.

The Rajneesh and the citizens lost trust in the judge for his poor judgment. He ended up leaving office under a cloud. It was a difficult time for him and his family. It was a point of honor for the elected and appointed officials in Wasco County that they upheld the law. The Rajneesh didn't realize that the elected officials were serious about serving the citizens and doing the best they could for them.

I can imagine the Rajneesh were quite upset with these bureaucrats who didn't know their place. To have to deal with such "low lifes" and have them deny their plans had to be galling to them. It was a "who do they think they are?" mentality on the ranch.

They didn't realize that the County Planner knew the laws and how to apply them. Land Use Laws in Oregon were well defined and well tested. Much of what the Rajneesh wanted to do had been litigated in the past and had been refused.

I was told that the Rajneesh, after the purchase, researched the land use laws in Oregon all the way back to when it became a territory in 1851. They tried all sorts of ways to use the laws in their favor.

When attempts like this and bribery didn't work, the Rajneesh tried intimidation. It worked, for a short time. In the end, those they were seeking to hurt dug in their heels. The Rajneesh sought to use tactics against people who don't scare, and who fight back if attacked. Instead of re-evaluating their methods, when the citizens pushed back, the Rajneesh pressed forward even harder.

CHAPTER 2

They didn't understand the people of Wasco County, or they wouldn't have tried their tactics on them. Honesty and a willingness to work with the county officials would have gone a long way to help their cause. While it would not have changed the outcome very much, they may have been allowed more housing units if the ranch was a working farm.

As they worked the land and showed that they were being successful but needed more people, more buildings would have been allowed. But that was not what they wanted.

They wanted a large commune capable of handling thousands of followers and were not interested in a smaller vision. They did not have any patience. Instead of downsizing their dream, or admitting their mistakes and trying to find another location, they chose to seek to humiliate, intimidate, and commit criminal acts of violence against those that were in opposition to their plan.

The television stations and media from Portland and other areas outside Wasco County seemed to thrive on the controversy. They would devote several minutes to the spokesperson, Sheela as she ranted and raved about the stupidity of citizens. Nothing was sacred to her. The best example was the treatment she gave a citizen who resided in Sherman County, just up the road from Antelope.

Sherman County was a smaller county, less than two thousand people, adjoining Wasco County. Most people drove on Highway 97 to get to Central Oregon, including Antelope and the ranch areas. The highway goes through Sherman County, so these citizens were also experiencing harassment and were concerned and outspoken against the Rajneesh.

This particular citizen had recently lost her husband in an accidental shooting. He had been hunting and made the fatal mistake of pulling his gun out of his rig barrel first. It went off and killed him.

A few days later Sheela was at a public meeting. Speaking directly into the television cameras she stated that this lady was a horrible, terrible person. Sheela stated that the woman was so bad even her husband couldn't stand her, so much so that he committed suicide to get away from her. Sheela finished it up with something to the effect that it was the truth. She always spoke the truth.

While I had seen some of these tactics and had heard from their victims, I had not experienced any of it firsthand until I ran for Office. I was not their ideal candidate. And they would do anything to keep me and the new commissioner from office, including murder.

The Wasco County election process in 1984 was a year of challenge and intrigue for everyone. Especially the County Clerk's office, who were responsible for elections in the county. But even before 1984, there was a vote on the City of Antelope ballot that created a stir around the county.

The Rajneesh despised the simple practicality of country life and the people that chose to live it. They conspired to upset as many citizens as they could and to coerce them into giving them what they wanted.

As individuals, they may not have thought about committing crimes. However, as a group they were conniving, relentless liars: vicious in their quest for a larger community where only cows were allowed. They wanted to set up a college and supporting businesses to promote the Rajneesh lifestyle.

They decided that they needed to have an incorporated city so they could make their own decisions regarding building and other issues. They set aside a portion of the ranch and started the process. Citizens in the adjoining acreage opposed them, as well as the county. This was zoned cattle/agriculture country, and the citizens wanted to keep it that way.

The County Commissioners of Wasco County, on advice of counsel, approved the request under extreme pressure from outside media. Locals appealed to the State. It should be noted that part of the ranch was located in Jefferson County to the south of Wasco County. They voted to refuse the request.

The long-time citizens of Antelope became concerned about their safety. Rajneesh followers moved in and demanded services that the city could not provide. Threats increased. The Rajneesh had several people in the sect that trained in the behavioral sciences, and they used their knowledge to set up confrontations. Citizens in Antelope and other small communities in the south part of the county experienced looking out their windows to find Rajneesh followers watching them for hours at a time.

Concerned citizens watched as followers took over the city government, driving them out. This small community of about twenty-six or so people concerned that the Rajneesh would take over, tried to dis-incorporate. The City Council felt it was necessary to dis-incorporate while the locals still outnumbered the Rajneesh. They felt the only way to save their way of life was to give up their right to be a town.

The drama and maneuvering that occurred foreshadowed the intriguing battle to come. The fight was on.

As Election Day approached, several Rajneesh moved into Antelope. They claimed citizenship by location. At that time, Oregon Voter laws allowed citizens to register to vote the day of elections. A law the Rajneesh used to their advantage.

They won the election, taking over the city government. There were a lot of changes in the city, which was renamed the City of Rajneesh. They made a point of changing all the street names to

Eastern Culture names, especially after Buddha and other gods. They named the city refuse area "Hitler" because they thought it was funny and appropriate to call the city dump by that name. Anything to mess with their conservative, ranching neighbors, not the least of which was a "Peace" force.

Because Antelope was so small and couldn't afford its own police department, Wasco County, and sometimes the Oregon State Police, would handle any calls for the town. Most citizens respected each other's privacy and, since it was considerably out of the way from major roads, had few visitors to cause any problems.

After the Rajneesh took over, they hired "peace officers" from the ranch to patrol the streets. The force consisted of armed Rajneesh stalking locals around the city. They patrolled at all hours and flashed spotlights into the citizens' windows, often after midnight and continuing until morning.

It was a form of harassment and intimidation. There was no need for the police department, nor did the town need to have AR-15s in addition to other costs. Most, but not all, of the costs and all of the officers, were covered by the ranch.

To the press, the Rajneesh stated they would be willing to exchange Antelope for the ability to have a city on the ranch. When the ranch was granted its citiship, they held onto Antelope. Some thought it was because the coercion didn't work; their childish spite rang true in everything they did. Citizens of Antelope were to endure the harassment and menacing behavior of these people until September of 1985.

Even though they now had two cities, the Rajneesh still had trouble with building permits and zoning laws. So they turned their attention to the next level of government: Wasco County.

The Rajneesh were most upset with the Wasco County Planning Office. They viewed the planner as their arch-enemy and started treating him as such. They harassed him whenever possible. Things were done to him that couldn't be attributed to the Rajneesh, but they were the only ones that had it out for him. He was genuinely concerned for his life and those of his family.

In January 1985 there was a fire in the Planning Office. It was arson. Someone(s) had placed candles in boxes soaked with an accelerant and then took off. It was right after midnight that someone driving by saw smoke and called 9-1-1. Part of the office was burned, computers were damaged. You know how I enjoy puns: when the Planning Director arrived at the office the first thing he asked of one of the investigators was, "Are my computers okay?" The answer: "Your computers are terminal."

Damage was done, but not irreparable. They had set up the timers, not all of which went off, and left the building. None of the windows were left open, so oxygen burned out early. Not as much damage was done as if they had let in air. We "knew" it was the Rajneesh, but there was no proof. There were others that were not happy with the Planning Office, but none so vehement.

The Commissioners put out a request for bids on the cleanup and rebuilding of the office. Several, including a submission from the Rajneesh, came in. A local contractor was the lowest bidder. Everyone breathed a sigh of relief. We all believed the Rajneesh would have set up some surveillance system in the office if they had the contract. Again, we couldn't prove it, but we "knew" it.

I do have to say that the Planning Director was one of the bravest men I knew. With all the threats made against him, he continued his job. The harassment got so bad at one point he sent his kids away for their own safety. When he went to the ranch to do his inspections he was accompanied by a deputy. The first time he came up to me and said that my predecessor had let him use a bulletproof vest, the Undersheriff pulled one out for him.

After a few times of this, I told him he was more than welcome to use it anytime. There was the fact that some of the weapons the Rajneesh had would go right through it. The poor guy just hung his head and wore it anyway. He never wavered and never let them intimidate him. He was afraid, but he did his job and did it very well.

To be honest, I really didn't think they would do something to him at the ranch; it would have undermined their claiming to be victims. While I had little doubt that they might hurt him, I thought it wouldn't be done on the ranch.

I was wrong in that thinking.

For a couple of years before the elections of 1984, I had been asked to run for the Office of Sheriff. As a commander with the City of The Dalles, I was well-known from my activities in the community. I worked hard, studied, trained, and did my job well. I had excellent management skills and ambition: all the things needed to be a good sheriff.

The citizens that urged me to run were very dissatisfied with the current sheriff. Many did not like how he was relating to the Rajneesh Cult in Southern Wasco County. They believed him too lenient on them. Some of those that approached me were afraid of the Rajneesh. The Rajneesh harassed and threatened these people, going as far as to display the weapons cache they stored on the ranch to these people.

The Rajneesh were well armed and made a point of displaying their weapons as they walked in front, beside and in back of the car driven by Bhagwan. While it was on their own property and perfectly legal, there was a message being sent out. "Don't mess with us down here," and, "We have the capability of action anywhere."

It wasn't the religion the citizens feared. It was the attitude of those in authority and what they were doing to control local government.

They felt the current sheriff, like some other elected officials, had been hoodwinked by these people. His lack of experience led to unaddressed problems. His background was as an engineer, not law enforcement. Before being elected, he'd served as a Reserve Deputy. With little to no real law enforcement or administrative experience, he relied on the advice of others to guide him. His deputies took advantage. Indeed, the Rajneesh also saw hesitancy and took advantage of it.

Early in the Sheriff's term, he had received bad advice from his supervisors. These decisions stretched to areas other than with the

Rajneesh. The total sum hurt the Office's credibility. There were some excellent law enforcement deputies in the Office, but several were less concerned with doing the work and more concerned about getting a paycheck. Some of these were in leadership positions. They became the anchor that pulled him down.

Personally, I liked the man. I felt he was honorable and doing his best. However, I also saw he was in over his head. The Office lacked discipline. It needed a professional demeanor.

One complaint was that the Sheriff's Office remained closed to the citizens. The Sheriff redacted reports before giving them to the press, even information on minor incidents.

There were no beginning of shift meetings since only a couple of people came on duty in the morning and evening. Shifts for patrol deputies and the rest of the staff fluctuated. The log was an efficient way of passing along info. Any department member wanting more information could get it by asking. It was simple to do, and important. It was the same log that we gave the news media to read; in doing so, we showed we had nothing to hide. When in the office I made time for the media, answering all questions with honesty.

Little things like opening this log to the press would become one of the many needed changes I made to the office. The first day one of the local newspapers came in and wanted to look at the log, it was given to him. He just glanced at it, smiled, and left. If only the previous sheriff had realized his mistake sooner. It might have saved him his job. Sadly, there was more to fix than accurate reports to the press.

Things had gotten so bad that at one point there was a move to recall the Sheriff. They asked if I would accept the office. I said no. What he did was not worthy of a recall. I am not sure how many others were approached, but I do know that after discussion they decided not to follow through. The general election was coming up in a few months. Change was on the horizon.

When I ran for Office in the spring of 1984, the Office of Sheriff was still a bi-partisan position. In my first term, it became a nonpartisan position by State Statute, the way it should be. I was a life-long Republican. My opponent was a Democrat.

Neither of us was opposed in the primary, so we ran against each other in the fall. I received a campaign check, right after the election in May, from the Republican Committee of Wasco County. I held onto it for almost a month. I didn't call my campaign committee together for that time.

I was having second thoughts. Among them was the fact I was running against a man who was already in the office and was seeking re-election. I came to the conclusion, after much discussion and prayer, that we needed a change. The system was set up to ensure the people had a say.

I felt God allowing me to be that person to do the changing. If not, I would not be elected. The more I got into the election process, the more I became aware of the problems. I went to meetings both large and small. Also, I did a lot of knocking on doors.

I was kind of well-known in the community. But not everyone knew me. I had a full beard. One door I knocked on had a young lady answer that thought I was a sannyasin from Rajneeshpuram. I had to show her my identification before she would talk to me. But most recognized me. Many said they knew my background and would be voting for me and recommending their family and friends do the same.

That summer was one of open hostility between the Rajneesh sect and members of the rest of the citizenry. The concern that they were trying to take over county government was a very real issue. They had done it once, they would do it again. The fear was that they would influence this particular election to further those goals. Nothing could be proven at the time, but mine wasn't the only gut with a bad feeling.

Bill went as far as to accuse the Rajneesh of attempted murder. He stated that he'd been poisoned on his visit to their compound. News channels ate him alive. They accepted the ridicule from the Rajneesh's side, posting on screens around the country. All the while ignoring the facts. The story changed from "Judge Poisoned" to "Local Official

Slandering Righteous Religious Group." The people of the county grew to despise the national media and the Rajneesh's lies on TV.

A political action committee was formed by some Wasco County residents. They supported some of us that were running. The people that organized the committee had been exposing the misdeeds of the Rajneesh for quite a while and felt those of us on the list were the most likely to not cave into their demands. The list was based on the people, not the party. Both Republicans and Democrats were represented.

Through the years, most elections in Wasco County were very close. One candidate was tied with another candidate for commissioner. After a recount, they flipped a coin. It was not unusual for the winner to win office by fewer than ten votes. One of my predecessors was elected by six votes more than his opponent.

Past practice of the Rajneesh, in elections, was everyone voted the same across the board. There may be one or two voters that didn't toe the line, but everyone else did. I believe at the time there were somewhere between five hundred and a thousand registered voters at Rajneeshpuram. It was enough to sway an election. Since they were a precinct onto themselves, their votes were visible.

Before that election took place, there was a lot of underhanded and criminal activity by the Rajneesh to swing the election their way. Having a large percentage of the vote wasn't enough. They wanted to guarantee a win. They were aware of how close most elections were in Wasco County and looked for ways to tip it in their favor.

They infiltrated the political action committee. Claiming to be a local resident against the Rajneesh, one young sannyasin joined and gained access to some of the committee's files. However, she was soon exposed. She went back down to the ranch.

Another young lady took up residence in The Dalles. She claimed she was a member of a long-standing family, the last of whom had moved from the area. However, she wanted to get back and help the county government by running for commissioner. She took out a petition to gain signatures that would put her on the ballot. She, too, was exposed. These infiltration tactics were just the start. The Rajneesh leadership planned more sinister actions to influence the election: Germ warfare.

CHAPTER 3

They had already poisoned a County Commissioner and County Judge by offering them water laced with Salmonella bacteria.

In the summer of 1984, the County Commissioners had taken their annual trip to the ranch to assess what was being done. On the way down they stopped at the little general store/cafe at Antelope. They were all given water to drink.

We later learned the Rajneesh placed the salmonella bacteria in the water of these two commissioners. The third official they felt was more inclined to support them so he received a germ-free glass. They, of course, didn't feel the effects right away.

They drove down to the ranch and parked their vehicle in the parking lot of the visitor center. They were then escorted around the ranch in one of the Rajneesh vehicles and told how the upcoming festival would be handled.

When they returned to their car, they found they had a flat tire. The weather was hot and changing the tire was hot and sweaty work. The County Judge was thirsty. All were offered water, but only the judge accepted. It was another glass of poison.

Both men got sick. The one who had only one dose was able to tough it out and, as he told me, "work through it." The County Judge almost lost his life. As he became very ill, he listened to his wife when she insisted he go to the hospital. That saved his life. In backtracking what he did and where he may have gotten the bacteria, he came to the conclusion that the Rajneesh had poisoned him. They denied it, and there was no proof.

The District Attorney of Jefferson County was also a victim who almost died from poisoning. I am still shaking my head over that fact. He had been a strong proponent of trying to work with them, but he also was a man of integrity and that might have been what upset them.

In September 1984 my wife Carla and I, along with our children, decided to go to Dufur and attend a potluck put on by the local citizens for anyone that was running for office. It was a campaign trip, but we enjoyed the people of Dufur. They were proof of small town hospitality.

We talked with people, left our cards and other election papers on the tables, along with those from several other politicians, and shook a lot of hands. We explained what we intended to do and how we intended to operate the Sheriff's Office once elected.

At the same time we were enjoying our meal and fellowship in Dufur, over 750 people were poisoned as they partook of various salad bars in restaurants throughout The Dalles.

Salmonella bacteria was introduced into the salad bars of these restaurants. Several ill people had to go to the hospital, most of them young or elderly. Visitors passing through also experienced the illness and hospitals up and down the Gorge had the same kind of patients: victims of the poisoning.

While no one that we were aware of died from the poisoning, many were ill and out of commission for weeks. Some even had permanent damage to their health and are still suffering the effects of the poison today, over 30 years later. The Public Health Dept. was called in and did an investigation. They called a poison control center in Atlanta and used personnel from the National services to attempt to run down the carrier.

There was a strong suspicion in The Dalles that the Rajneesh had somehow tainted the vegetables in the salad bars, but there was no proof. Later, we learned that at least one grocery store had also been attacked by a follower pouring the bacteria over fresh vegetables.

There was no common carrier found. The reason given for the mass illness was servers in the various restaurants were not taking proper sanitary precautions. While it was very strange and quite a "coincidence" that all of the restaurants had the same problem at the same time, no other reason could be attributed to the outbreak, or so the National service decided.

Most of the restaurants, through no fault of their own, lost their business. They had been sued and lost a lot of patrons. Damage wasn't just to those that became ill but impacted many businesses and their employees as they were accused of improper sanitation and lost their jobs. The financial implications for all the victims were high and can never be calculated.

In fairness to the National office, they had never encountered anything like this before, and there was no proof of a direct attack. Without the ability to issue search warrants on mere suspicion they couldn't force a search of the Rajneesh compounds, so even if they had determined it was a deliberate attack it would have been almost impossible to make a case.

It was a test run. The Rajneesh felt that if they poisoned people, then fewer would go to the polls on Election Day, and it would be enough for them to have their candidates win the election. However, not enough people got sick from the salad bars and now, due to their experiment, you couldn't find a salad bar in The Dalles anyway. To this day, many Wasco County residents will never go to a restaurant with a buffet.

Since the salad bar poisoning didn't seem to be enough to keep voters from the polls, the Rajneesh looked at poisoning The Dalles' water system.

One of the things they considered was to place a beaver in a commercial blender, grind it up, and deposit the remains into the water system. The beavers can carry a germ called Giardiasis and it acts on the intestines much as salmonella does.

But the water system was well protected, and they would not be able to get enough poison into the system to be dangerous – so they gave up on that idea.

The Rajneesh also smeared poison on door knobs in the County Court House, but nothing came of it, and we didn't know about it until much later.

Just when they decided on the next measure to sway the election and who the primary engineer of the idea was I am not sure. They put together a plan to bring several men and a few women that were homeless onto the ranch. Allegedly a humanitarian measure, in truth they thought they could control them and convince them to vote as the Rajneesh directed in the upcoming election.

One has to wonder what these people were thinking. They were not stupid people. However, they didn't have much common sense. And they didn't have much experience in working with people that they considered beneath their social status.

They were very naïve in many ways. Thinking they could bring in busloads of homeless and give them direction was absolute idiocy. They had no clue what they were about to get into.

Most of the people they gathered from the biggest cities in America were street people because they refused to conform to society. There may have been a few that welcomed an opportunity to better themselves and get off the street, but there were few, if any.

Many were mentally ill, some addicted to alcohol or other drugs, while others were very independent. These people would no more be controlled by the Rajneesh than they were by the rest of society. All were either outcast from society or chose to rebel against society.

There was a trailer park near the railroad in The Dalles where a number of hobos regularly camped. One day I stopped by the park, as I often did, and started talking with some of the hobos. One, in particular, was always good for conversation. This man lived in a small travel trailer about 10 feet long from the late 40's or early 50's.

The wheels had been taken off, and the trailer was on blocks. It was his bed and shelter from the weather. He lived his life outside in the small fenced in yard, about 50 to 60 square feet.

This was where this man fixed his meals, ate, and entertained his guests: other hobos. There was no running water: he got it from a faucet down the road. And no indoor plumbing. Let's leave it at that.

His was one of four or five that were still around at that time. There had been others as well, set up by the Railroad to allow workers to sleep in between assignments for a day or two. They were not meant to be permanent housing, only sleeping quarters.

Those remaining became houses for hobos. They paid about $20 a month to stay there. One of these men had been arrested for some misdemeanor within the city. He was brought before the Municipal Court judge for arraignment.

The young man that was sitting in as the judge that day was a first-year law student that interned with an attorney. The attorney, as the appointed judge, let the young man experience a courtroom as a judge pro-tem.

The defendant pled not guilty. The judge asked if he could afford an attorney and the defendant said no.

So the judge started asking him questions about his finances so he could appoint an attorney. When it came to his residence, the defendant said he lived at the Railroad Trailer Park.

The judge asked him, "What is your rent?" The defendant said, "$20.00."

The judge asked, "Is that by the day or week?" The defendant replied, "By the month."

A puzzled look came across the judge's face, and he looked at me. I just nodded my head. He continued to fill out the form, and the defendant was taken back to jail to talk with his court-appointed attorney.

I took the judge by the trailer court after court. He said something like, "I had no idea people lived like this."

As it happened this day, the conversationalist and another hobo were talking. He said that some "social worker" was trying to get him to move into the Commodore Apts. This was an apartment complex located in the middle of town and built in the early 1920's. It was kind of run down. It was one of the few places where those on a limited income could afford to live.

Many of the residents of the Commodore were also outcasts, and there was a lot of criminal activity connected with those that resided there. It was right across from the Police Station, so at least it was close by for our responses.

He looked at his guest and me, and he said, "Why would I want to move into town and give up all this?" as he gestured around him.

He had some limited income. I'm not sure how much or from what. He lived quite comfortably in that trailer. Had the Rajneesh approached him he would probably have let them know in no uncertain terms he was not interested.

However, his friend that day might have been if it promised three meals and a warm bed; three hots and a cot, in colloquial terms. His camp was on the outskirts of town in a small clump of trees. He was almost always intoxicated and could be a mean drunk if confronted by what he considered any hostility.

Neither of these people could be easily controlled by others. These were the kind of individuals that were scooped up and promised a better life at the ranch. When the homeless arrived at the ranch, they were required to register to vote. The Rajneesh thought that they could later control how they voted, or probably vote for them without their knowledge. They were not above doing just that: they had complete control of the ballot box at the ranch.

The newcomers underwent physical tests, including tests for diseases. They were given plastic wrist bracelets to designate what they would be allowed to do while on the ranch. One color allowed them to stay at the ranch in a more confined area. Another enabled them to mingle. Yet another showed they were disease free and could have sex with the other people at the ranch.

It didn't take long before it became apparent that the street people were going to present problems for the ranch. Therefore, it also wasn't long before the doctors were ordering large amounts of Haldol, a tranquilizer, to control their behavior.

We were told that there was more Haldol used in Rajneeshpuram while the street people were there than all of the rest of Oregon put together. Not much doubt about what it was being used for, but since it was administered by medical personnel the state didn't look into it, and we didn't become aware until much later. Not much doubt in my mind that it was over prescribed and violated the law, but that became a mute issue.

As a publicity stunt, the Rajneesh decided to bring a couple of busloads of the street people into town to hand-deliver registration forms to the county courthouse. They announced their intent and made sure the news media knew when they would be there. Not only was the local press there, but news media from the Portland area were also there with TV cameras.

The courthouse was a beehive of activity as the Rajneesh and the street people walked in. You could hardly move in the courthouse, so many news people and others were trying to take it in.

The Rajneesh were getting the results they thought they wanted as cameras focused on them.

I had the day off, but I wanted to see what would happen. I became part of that crowd, but stood off a ways, on the landing of the stairs going up to the third floor. We did have officers and deputies in the building and outside to handle disturbances if necessary.

I don't remember if Sheela was part of the group or not. It would

27

have been unusual if she was not. However, the Rajneesh escorted the street people into the Courthouse. Prancing before the cameras with big smiles on their faces, the attitude was evident: "We will show the locals that you can't mess with the Rajneesh." They were enjoying their charade as they told the press what they were doing.

They had no idea!

They worked their way through the crowd towards the Clerk's Office. At that time the County Clerk and the Oregon Secretary of State came out of the Clerk's Office and stood side by side in front of the door.

They then announced that from this point on all newly registered voters in the county would undergo a challenge and had to prove they had been in the county the required amount of time to vote in local elections and that they were legally registering. The emphasis was on "all." There were always people who changed addresses or had name changes, etc. that had to re-register to vote. The State law had been changed after the Antelope fiasco where people could register and vote the same day, to a length of time in residency within the county. Any of those would also have to go through the challenge.

Also because of acts of spite and harassment, many citizens had to come in because "someone" had said they had moved and sent in registration forms to that effect. So they had to re-establish their residency.

The street people did not meet the timeline. They had come to the ranch too late. There were a couple of street people that shouted against the action, claiming a violation of their rights, and the Rajneesh were very upset. One street person ranted and raved before the cameras that he was a veteran and that he had fought for the right to vote.

The Rajneesh were claiming a conspiracy and that the action was illegal. They were a "bit" upset. Angrily they left the courthouse, ranting, and raving and vowing to sue. They had been outmaneuvered, and they knew it. They had egg all over their faces and didn't like it.

I would have loved to have been a fly in their vehicles and their meeting rooms back at the ranch. I am sure some interesting comments were made. There was lots of drama, but the "superior intelligence" sources of the Rajneesh had made some severe errors, and they were being exposed as the conniving, "win at all costs" people they were. There was more to come.

Meanwhile, Larry Ann Willis, the Democrat candidate running for the US Congress in our district, filed suit. She stated that the Rajneesh were a corporation illegally using funds for campaign purposes when they drove people to the courthouse to register as voters. No more buses came up from the ranch with people to record.

Ms. Paulus arranged to have hearings for contested registrations to be held at the local armory. She had some volunteers, mostly attorneys, come into The Dalles as hearings officers to preside over individual meetings with citizens. The interviews were conducted in plenty of time for the voters to clarify their status.

There were a few voters who had to change their registration for whatever reason, they had moved and needed to update their address being the most frequent reason.

However, there were also registration cards that were sent in by someone other than the citizen it was supposed to be from. More harassing techniques perpetrated by the Rajneesh. It ended up not interfering with the election process. Those few citizens affected came into the armory to get the situation corrected. To be sure, they were not happy, especially those that had someone tinker with their registration, but they did it.

None of the Street people staying at Rajneeshpuram showed up. It became apparent to the Rajneesh that their ploy wasn't going to work, and they had no use for these people. They were a drag on the ranch and few if any were productive. So one Wednesday night, right before the election, busses loaded with these people were brought into The Dalles, Madras, and Portland. They dropped them off to fend for themselves. It was yet another stab at the local government since everything else with the street people plot failed.

The Police Department patrolled the area and made sure there were no problems. In The Dalles, volunteers were called on. The Red Cross and Salvation Army set up at the Salvation Army to give out clothes, blankets, food, and bus tickets to Portland. Portland was more equipped to handle these people, and many of them came from there. Our town cared for these people. And they sent them on their way with a minimum of disruption to the citizens of The Dalles.

The election itself became uneventful. There was almost a 100% turn out to vote. Those supported by the Political Action Committee won by a wide margin.

Were all the street people sent away, or did some remain at the ranch, cremated, their ashes scattered in the hills? Don't know. They didn't keep records.

CHAPTER 4

was elected in early November 1984. However, I was not to take office until January 7th, 1985. The current sheriff, whom I had defeated, allowed me to come into the office and get oriented. He allowed me to go wherever I wanted or felt I needed to go without restriction, even taking the time to go over some of his concerns he thought I would have to address when I was sworn into the office. I appreciated that. He could have just as well told me no. As I said earlier, he was a good guy, but not prepared to handle the position.

I had been a City Police Officer, and I was good if I do say so myself. I worked with a strong team of men and women, under strong leadership from our Chief, and we functioned well. The police department focused on enforcing the law. The officers issue tickets, become mediators in the family and other disputes, make arrests and investigate crimes. As the director in charge of Crime Prevention, I built an active volunteer organization from the ground up. It was one of the reasons so many people knew me.

I had always been aware of public relations and the need to relate to the citizens. I spoke at meetings, and I was frequently in the schools talking to students about law enforcement, listening to them, and talking about how we worked. I spoke to kindergarten through high school classes often, on my own time. I also spoke on career days. Teachers would request my help when they wanted a police officer's perspective of the Constitution and the responsibility of the citizens.

I had some administrative duties, but mainly my position of Commander was more supervisory than administrative. I took classes in both the private and law enforcement section on management and regulations concerning employees, as well as criminal law. I subscribed to management periodicals to help me improve my performance as a Commander. Those contacts I made over the years, as well as the classes I took, helped me perfect my professional abilities. So when the opportunity presented itself, I felt ready for the Office of Sheriff.

In many ways I was. I knew the criminal law and the application of it as a police officer. I understood the responsibility of a manager and leader and was prepared to take that task on.

But a Police Department was a lot different from a Sheriff's Office. While I knew what the responsibilities of a sheriff were, I had a lot to learn about the application of those duties.

While the Sheriff's Offices did the same job as the City's Police Departments, we had many additional duties: Service of several thousand civil papers a year, and you had to have a good civil deputy. Fortunately, we did. We later had another clerk cross-trained to take over on her vacations. The clerk assigned as Civil Deputy told me she appreciated that. For the first time, she was able to go on vacation or take a few days off without worrying about what might happen at the office. Serving of papers, making sure they were done in a timely manner and recorded correctly, as well as making sure they were the correct forms was a serious issue and failure to do the job right could cost the county money and embarrassment for the Sheriff's Office.

This became especially important in our dealings with the Rajneesh since a large percentage of the papers to serve involved them. Usually failure to pay, etc.

In the spring of 1985, activity from the Rajneesh increased: the leaders were "back in town."

The courthouse had an alarm system with security buzzers set up, terminating in the Sheriff's Office. They had been installed after some of the Rajneesh had been creating scenes in various buildings. In 1985 a system like this was unheard of. I didn't know of any other county courthouse in the state that had a similar alarm. Of course, they are more prevalent now. Almost all have something similar, including metal detectors, etc.

We received a buzz from the County Judge's office one morning. A sergeant and I quickly went upstairs to find three (maybe four) Rajneesh in the secretary's office. The office was about six feet by fifteen, or so, long and narrow. They were loudly proclaiming they had a records request, and they wanted it right then. The secretary was in distress at all the yelling.

They were loud and pushy. Right after we came into the office we watched the County Judge go to a filing cabinet and say he thought the information was there. As he opened the drawer, a Rajneesh shoved him aside in an attempt to search it herself. As I mentioned before, I knew the laws concerning most public administrative actions, as well as criminal law.

I told the Judge to close the drawer and go into his office. He looked at me and complied. The person who had been trying to get into the file drawer sought to follow. The Sergeant grabbed her arm, detaining her. She started yelling police brutality. The Judge closed the door.

I told her to knock it off and then turned to the secretary. I asked her if she had the written request. She did. Was it understandable? Yes. Can you have it ready by tomorrow morning? Yes.

While public records were available to the public, that didn't mean "right now." The department had the right to do it when they had time, or when they could have someone come in to find and make necessary copies of the requested documents. I then told her to tell the Rajneesh she has all she needs and that she would have it available tomorrow. All of this was in front of them, of course. She told them. I then told her to tell them their business was finished, and they needed to leave.

They started throwing a fit, three years olds that they were. "This is a public office," they said. "We have a right to be here, we want the information now."

I told them that either they left now, or I was going to arrest them for criminal trespass. After a few seconds, during which they realized I was serious, they decided to go. The secretary was grateful. I went into the Judge Bill's office and talked with him.

I had contacts with Bill on a regular basis because of events like this, sometimes several times a week. A quiet man, he spoke with the authority of wisdom, experience, and confidence. He loved people, and his desire to serve the citizens of Wasco County to the best of his ability remained present at all times. He treated everyone, including the Rajneesh, equally and it grieved him that they didn't see that he was genuinely interested in them.

The Rajneesh saw his gentleness as weakness, and his patience as a thing to be despised made fun of and exploited. Bill didn't wear his Christianity on his sleeve, but it didn't take long to see that Christ did indeed live within him. Christ was his strength as he went through these and other challenges in his terms of office.

I remember one time, not sure how we started the conversation, but he told me that he had some bad years as a Wheat Rancher (all farmers can give that same story). One year he had to borrow money from the bank to pay tithe to his church. It was said matter of fact. No fanfare, boasting or thumping of his chest. Just a statement made on how he fulfilled that obligation.

It's hard to explain how that statement impacted me. It wasn't meant as a lesson. It wasn't a teaching moment. It was just a statement of fact by a Christian who had Christ living within him to another Christian. By the time of this conversation, I had learned to appreciate Bill, his wisdom, and his service to Christ. This lifted Bill to a whole new level in my eyes.

I understood and appreciated his position. However, I recommended that he use the hallway going from the lobby of the courthouse to his offices as a waiting room. He didn't want to do that. Bill understood, though, that if he didn't then more incidents like this would happen. He also understood that he had to treat everyone in the county the same. Even his good friends and neighbors would have to wait to be allowed into the offices.

This actually distressed him. He wanted to treat the Rajneesh like any other citizen, but they wouldn't let him. While I was talking to him one of the Rajneesh came back to the office and told me that their attorney wanted to speak with me. In the lobby of the courthouse was a pay phone and she had called back to the ranch. While under no obligation, I chose to talk with the person. I was interested in what she would say.

I went to the phone, and the lawyer started threatening me. Telling me I couldn't kick her people out, what we were doing was illegal, and they would file charges, etc. After listing to her diatribe for a minute or so, I asked, "Are you a criminal attorney?" She didn't answer.

Knowing by her response, she wasn't, I asked her again, "Are you a criminal attorney?" Again she didn't answer.

I said, "I would strongly suggest you contact a criminal attorney because if any of them go back into that office they will be arrested and you can come up and bail them out of the jail."

There was a pause on the other end, and then she asked to speak to the leader of that group. I stood back and watched. After a couple minutes, she hung up, gave me a dirty look, and they all stomped off. Bill did as I suggested. The other offices either already had a set up where the public couldn't pass without permission, or soon installed something. We never again had an incident of that kind in any of the offices in the courthouse. That didn't stop the Rajneesh from trying other things, though.

The Jail, Animal Control, and dispatching, contract with federal and state governments to have extra patrol on the county's forest and BLM, lands as well as on the waterways. Our patrol area was two thousand four hundred square miles as compared to the seven square miles in the city. We were responsible for Search and Rescue, and while we didn't experience a lot of calls, we had to respond and deal with them, and we didn't have a team.

In the Police Department, I had the responsibility of running a few programs and shifts. Two other Commanders and I advised the Chief, who worked with the City Manager in the operation of the agency.

While the Police Chief was indeed the head of the department, the City Manager had to approve all decisions he made. The Chief was given a lot of free reign but, in the end, he wasn't the final authority.

In the city, the City Council had direct authority over the City Manager, and while they were not allowed to have direct disciplinary contact with the employees, they could direct the City Manager to take disciplinary or discharge action.

There were a lot of levels between myself and the finalization of policies and procedures, personnel issues, etc. It was much different for an elected sheriff.

As sheriff, chosen by the citizens, I answered directly to the citizens. I learned early on when I asked another elected official for advice about something that "elected representatives don't tell other elected officials what to do." While that wasn't entirely accurate, it pretty well defined my role in the county.

When I first came to orient myself with the Sheriff's Office, the Sheriff showed me a letter of complaint he had received against one of the deputies from the Rajneesh Chief of Police. He said he got these all the time. I asked if he was going to answer. He said no.

The letter ended with how wonderful it was to be a Chief of Police in a crime-free community that was so much greater than what we had to see. It was a typical statement, he said, and it came in every letter. I only had a few letters that came into my Office from the Chief in regards to my deputies' actions. I always answered them.

I remembered one, in particular, that came in concerning a deputy's driving too fast on the county road going through the property. It seems that he was driving along the road, and one of the Rajneesh was driving in front of him, "adhering to the speed limit of 25." The deputy had the nerve to pass the Rajneesh and put everyone's life in danger.

I talked to the deputy. He said that the car was going around 15 to 20 mph, but where he passed her was in a wide spot in the road, and he had plenty of room and visibility to pass safely. He believed the driver was intentionally trying to slow him down and interfere with him.

This was not an isolated incident. In prior years it used to happen often. Once they "arranged" for a truck to have an accident and block the road just before the County Planner was supposed to do inspections. He was held up for several hours.

I wrote back to the Chief that I had discussed it with my deputy. He told me that the car was going too slow and was hampering him in his official duties. He was able to pass her in a safe location and did so safely. I also told her if we had any further incidents of this nature the deputies were instructed to issue citations and/or make arrests. We never had another incident of that nature.

I found, at least in things involving my Office, that if we were able to show that we knew what we were talking about and were willing to take action, they backed off.

I answered to the County Commissioners in as much as how my activities affected the county. However, they could not tell me what I could or could not do in the Office. As long as I obeyed the laws they had no say in my Office, except when it came to budgeting.

We had to submit our budgets to a budget committee made up of the three elected commissioners and three private citizens appointed by the commissioners. They could control some of what we did by either withholding or give funds to operate the Office.

I knew what the Office was all about, but I had a lot to learn about the operation of the Office and how it interacts with the citizens. When I received my driver's, permit I had yet to drive a car. I was bragging to a friend that I had aced my test. His comment was, "But that doesn't mean you can drive." In short, I was too cocky.

Same point.

CHAPTER 5

had been elected, but I needed time in the Office to learn how to be sheriff. And there was a lot to learn. While I knew there were problems within the Office, I found there were far more than I had known and some were dangerous to the deputies and the county as a whole. I had a lot more work to do than I had appreciated.

My objectives for the Office when I was running for the Office were to professionalize the department; provide more training for employees, with more accountability for actions; meaningful evaluations; and weeding out management staff that was ineffective, giving them an opportunity to prove themselves to me. Open communications with the media and citizens were also important. There was also dealing with conflicts between the Rajneesh and other citizens of Wasco County, more presence in the south part of the county, and more volunteer programs.

The citizens also had some objectives for us. Dealing with the Rajneesh was far and away number one priority for them, followed by more visibility throughout the county of both the deputies and the sheriff.

Once elected, however, I started re-evaluating what I thought needed to be done. Some of it was because of what I was seeing while orienting to the office, and some was mandated by law. In addition to the above, I had to add other objectives. A countywide 9-1-1 program had to be completed by the end of 1985, and we were a long way off from meeting that requirement. The jail had some serious personnel and operational issues, in addition to being a substandard facility with an attorney lurking around who was keen to sue us on behalf of the inmates. Some of the supervisors just needed more training, and we needed to get them on the same page with me. Others were just incompetent, or acted in an adversarial manner, and I would have to document their mishaps because a lot had been allowed under the previous sheriff. I felt I was going to have to create a new standard for the Office. That was going to take a longer time than I had originally thought. We were going to have to go from a slack office to a more regimented and professional Office. I was going to face resistance. Dealings with the Rajneesh were much more involved than I had been appraised of initially

In that first year, I had to add Rajneesh investigation to the list. Fortunately, the State Police and the Attorney General's Office were the chief investigators, and while at first, I didn't appreciate them taking point, it became obvious we couldn't handle it at our small county level.

It was hard to prioritize my objectives, mainly because so many were very important, and in other lists each would have been priority one.

But my first surprise came during a County Commissioner's meeting on December 2nd before I took Office. It dealt with the Rancho Rajneesh's festival the next summer and became my priority even before taking office. It was my first taste of the world which revolved around the Rajneesh.

I was in the Sheriff's Office on December 2nd when I was told that this was one of those days that the County Court was holding a regular Commissioners meeting. On the agenda was the Rajneesh Summer Festival for the last week of June and the first week of July 1985. In Oregon, if you have a meeting of over three thousand people in an area not otherwise authorized, you must obtain a permit from the governmental entity that oversees the location.

The Rajneesh scheduled a celebration every year since their arrival at the ranch. The festival was centered on the birth date of Bhagwan Shree Rajneesh. It would reportedly bring in about 15,000 people to the Ranch.

However, throughout the summer they would have seminars that members could attend. Some came before the celebration, staying for the celebration and leaving afterward. Others would come for the celebration and stay for some of the seminars afterward. The celebration would take about two weeks. So people would be coming in slowly most of the time and the population would gradually build.

I went upstairs to the Circuit Court Room where the Commissioners' meeting was being held that day. I came in through the back and observed. The courtroom was packed out with every bench filled with Rajneesh and other citizens, and the walls lined with people. I had heard that this would be the case. It always was when the Rajneesh had an issue before the County Commissioners.

I had been told that the Rajneesh would come in and take over the first few rows of seating. If there were other citizens there, they would force their way onto the benches and eventually force the other citizens off.

This day was not any different. Some other citizens had arrived early and taken seats, the Rajneesh attempted their usual aggressive seating. But this time, it was not working as well. There were a lot of determined faces on the other citizens of the county, and they did not budge.

The Rajneesh were demanding that the County Commissioners make a decision on the Festival Permit that day. The other citizens were opposed to the decision being made that day and wanted it tabled until the new County Commissioner took office.

As the commissioners listened to both sides, they decided to table the discussion of the issuance of the permit until the next meeting. That meeting would be held the last week of December and just before the other Commissioner was sworn into office. The Rajneesh were very upset.

As I turned to leave the room, the District Attorney came up to me and said, "You know that you have to approve the security for the festival, don't you?"

"No!" I said. This was a real surprise to me. I had no idea that I would have to approve security measures, and I didn't have the slightest idea what their measures consisted of.

"You can just approve what they are doing. It will be the same as it was in years past," he said.

I was not about to put my stamp of approval on security arrangements I had no idea about. I went down to the Sheriff's Office, and the Sheriff confirmed I would have to approve the festival. "We never had any problems down there," he said.

However, there had been a death during each of the prior two festivals. One was an older and very ill man who came in by ambulance so he could die in the presence of Bhagwan. The other was a young man who had attended the previous year and had drowned on the John Day River while rafting. Because of those deaths, and the history of less than cooperative behavior from the Rajneesh, I wanted a good look at the security plans and then I had some conditions I wanted to be met.

When people come from all over the world and are unfamiliar with water safety, accidents can happen. At that time, I had no reason to believe the death was anything other than an accident. But I was wary.

I talked with the Commissioners and told them I had some concerns about the festival security and would be submitting a list of conditions to be met before I signed off on it. I then went home and began making the list. With fifteen thousand additional people in the valley and only the narrow road serving it, I wanted to be sure there would be nothing blocking the road. One of the conditions to be met was to have a tow truck on site and ready to remove any vehicles if an accident should occur during the festival. I would not have my staff, or other emergency personnel kept from going into the area for any reason.

I knew that when an official wanted to contact someone at the Ranch it could be very difficult. The Rajneesh made sure that people could be hard to find, and deputies and other county officials would waste time trying to find them.

The Sheriff's Office was continually serving civil papers on the Commune, often being stonewalled. I understand they had over one hundred and fifty separate corporations set up. The corporate offices were located in the office complex above the mall. Each corporation had a designated location within the office. For example, one might be the top drawer of the fifth desk in the third row. Then if no one was at the desk at the moment, the deputy had to wait until they came back. It was a game the Rajneesh enjoyed playing.

It was also difficult to get in touch with the Police Chief, a fact I had already found out. Therefore, I also wanted to include the condition that the Chief of Police would be available to me twenty-four hours a day during the festival, and that she would return any and all of my calls within twenty minutes.

I told them I would not work with a reserve or a security person. It had to be the Chief, who I knew would be there the entire time. Because the population would increase over the course of the festival, I requested a daily count of people coming onto the ranch beginning June 20th.

Someone from the Police Department was to call my office each morning by 8:00 am and give us a count. I had a good idea of just about when people would arrive, but the daily census would help confirm the population growth. Since the visitors had to travel through the county, it allowed me to schedule personnel accordingly. It also gave me an indication of the numbers on the ranch at any given time.

There were other conditions concerning the safety of the visitors. The last thing concerned the weaponry they had on the ranch. For some time I had been told the Rajneesh had automatic weapons, there were even those that swore they saw a mounted machine gun on the helicopter that flew over the route that Bhagwan drove over every day.

I knew that ammunition for various weapons for the rest of Oregon was in short supply, and some dealers had shipped truckloads of ammo to the ranch. Therefore, I also wanted the count and type of weapons available to them during the festival and how much ammo they possessed.

I ran the conditions by the District Attorney and informed the Commissioners I would like to present it to them during the next meeting as consideration for requirements for the permit.

I was on the agenda for the meeting. I presented my list of conditions for my approval to the County Commissioners, who in turn gave it to the Rajneesh. The Commissioners endorsed my list.

The Rajneesh challenged my standing as the Sheriff-Elect and my right to make conditions since I was not the sheriff. One of the commissioners pointed out that I would be taking office shortly, I would be the sheriff during the festival, and therefore the conditions were to be met. The Rajneesh were not happy.

They were also told that the decision of whether to issue the permit was postponed until the new commissioner was sworn into office in a couple of weeks.

The Rajneesh were very upset. They wanted the permit approved now. In fact, they were demanding it be approved. The commissioners were well within their rights to postpone the vote and didn't budge.

The Rajneesh were concerned because the new Commissioner had originally resigned his office. He had been advised to rule for the Rajneesh over specific issues and resigned in protest.

The commissioner that had lost the election frequently voted for the Rajneesh. I knew him well. He was an honest man that had a Christmas Tree Farm and with whom I had many occasions to talk. He voted as he did out of a sense of right. While many felt he had become a pawn of the Rajneesh, he was not. While I too didn't agree with all his votes, he was not devious.

The other two commissioners were not so favorably impressed

with the Rajneesh. The Rajneesh were concerned that if one of them chose not to vote for the festival, they would lose on a possible 2-1 vote. These were the two commissioners they poisoned the previous summer.

In the end, the permit was issued. They hemmed and hawed for several weeks, but finally came up with the conditions I required. One of my sergeants met with their security people and was satisfied that they had an acceptable plan.

They also had to meet conditions for the Planning and Health Departments: all those conditions were met.

They didn't want to give me a weapons or ammo count, but I used their tactic of submitting a "public information request" and received an inventory. I knew that I had no way of verifying the information and that it probably wasn't completely accurate, but we at least had an idea of what was on the ranch.

There were no automatic weapons listed, nor any "machine gun" attached to the helicopter. It would not necessarily have been unlawful for them to possess automatic weapons. As long as the federal firearms laws are followed, anyone may possess an automatic weapon. But they only listed semi-auto rifles and handguns, revolvers, bolt action rifles and pump action shotguns. Pretty standard issue for Police agencies.

Our deputies told me that they thought it was a fairly accurate depiction of the weaponry they had seen at the ranch. They had not seen a weapon on the helicopter, nor had they ever seen any automatic weapons. I had no reason not to approve the security and did so. I later regretted not making one more condition. It wouldn't happen again.

CHAPTER 6

had never been to the Rajneesh ranch prior to becoming sheriff. I had thought about doing it while campaigning, but I just didn't have time to drive that distance to court a group that had made it clear they didn't want any changes in the Sheriff's Office.

The population of that ranch was fluid. Some say it was around 2000 permanent residents. In the winter months, my deputies estimated that there couldn't be much over one hundred or so. They based that opinion on activity when they served papers and the tracks in the snow: not many. It was just a guess, but they felt there just wasn't very many people down there at that time.

That later became a factor when one of the leaders admitted they didn't often hold council meetings and just made up the minutes. I imagine they didn't have enough of the council to have a quorum. The Rajneesh fudged numbers, a lot. They were always stating they had more followers there and worldwide than they could prove. They needed to project an image of strength.

After I had been elected, I felt I needed to make contact, particularly with the Police Chief. I knew all my counterparts in the immediate area, but I had never met her. I had been trying for several weeks to set up this meeting with the city of Rajneesh's Chief of Police. I had written her a letter when I could not contact her by phone. I wanted to meet her to establish a professional relationship, as I had with other chiefs and sheriffs close to or adjoining our county. She continually replied the Mayor was out of town and unavailable.

I told her while I would like to meet the Mayor, I wanted to meet with her as the chief. I had never encountered any chief that had to have a mayor with them to meet with another law enforcement official. But I also knew that this "city" was different and ran differently than any other city in the United States. It was under the operations directive of the religion. She would not relent and insisted the Mayor be there. Finally, we were able to set up a meeting in the middle of March, with the mayor.

I had arisen early that morning. As it happened, it was the same day as our weekly Christian Emergency Service Providers Breakfast. I asked prayer for wisdom. I left the breakfast feeling at peace, stopped by my office for a moment, exchanged my car for a Chevy Blazer, and started the long trek to the ranch. I would be on the road for about 2-3 hours before I arrived at the Police Department. Most of the trip was on paved state roads.

It was a relatively easy drive until I left Shaniko, a ghost town, and started down the hill, with lots of switchbacks, into Antelope, then called Rajneeshpuram. I went through Antelope and then southeast towards the county road that went through the ranch. They knew I was coming, of course, but we also knew that the Rajneesh followers watched us when we drove through that City and called to the ranch to let them know they could be expecting visitors. So I knew they had called ahead to let the ranch know that I was on my way.

I took the turn off onto the county road. While gravel, the road was bladed and in good condition. It was actually wider than the state roads in that area. This road had a lot of use from the local ranchers, and now the Rajneesh.

I turned onto the narrower county road that went through the ranch. This road goes from Wasco to Jefferson County and then Wheeler County, coming out near Fossil. However, it was rarely used by anyone other than those living at the ranch. It was getting heavier use now, though, from the Rajneesh, the vendors, the curious and of course, the County Agencies.

At the border to the ranch was an open gate and a few feet inside was a guard post. They called them "information posts". They were about 6'X6', as I recall, and fully enclosed. The top portion was glass, the bottom metal. There was a total of four spaced a mile or two apart, on the road down to the city.

They had a pullout area next to the road so people could pull over and talk to the guards. The stated purpose by the Rajneesh was this was an information booth so they could let visitors know about road conditions. But we had been informed by some citizens that they would try and discourage anyone from driving any further down the road.

The road was a county road and open to the public. No permission was needed to drive on it, yet many people thought they had to stop at the guard shack and get permission to go further. The Security people did all they could to support that misconception and to discourage people from traveling the road. The commune did not welcome uninvited guests.

There were two followers standing at the guard shack. They were security personnel clad in a maroon uniform, with brown leather police utility belts consisting of the normal security/police items. I had been told they had semi-automatic weapons also in the shack, but if they did the weapons must have been behind the metal panels since they were not visible.

I smiled and waved to them as I drove by. They both raised their hands shoulder high, waving hesitantly. A look of surprise that I would acknowledge them that way.

While I had not been down this road before, I knew the procedure. Many of the deputies and officials had been blocked and slowed down or even stopped for a period of time as they had driven down this road. Accidents were staged, cars driven slowly and could not be passed on the narrow road. Anything to slow the deputy and other county employees.

They had not been physically molested or threatened, at least not on the road. And no one could prove the actions of Rajneesh's followers were deliberate, but we knew they were. There were too many coincidences.

The Security personnel knew just how long it should take to travel between each post. As someone passed a post his/her vehicle and occupancy information was called down to the next post.

If the traveler was not at the next post within the proper time frame, a security person was sent to find out why. If the visit was a surprise and the group had not prepared for the arrival of officials, they would somehow use those methods stated above to slow things down until they were ready. They were in control, or at least they liked to give the illusion of being in control of the road.

The road was a county road and therefore public. However, most of the property bordering the road belonged to the commune. All 64,000 acres, 100 square miles of it. To be sure, there were several thousand more acres of public BLM land, but if a person intended to go off the county road he had better know how to read a map. The security force was not forgiving and would have taken legal action if their property was trespassed on. They unsettled the citizens as they drove down this road.

In many places the road was only 8 to 10 feet wide, going between a steep hill on one side and a deep ravine on the other. In a few places, the road would widen out to 20 feet or so for a few yards. It was designed by the county so a vehicle going one direction could pull over and wait for oncoming traffic to pass. The speed limit for the entire way was 25 miles per hour so drivers would have time to react to anything coming up. In some areas, it was the best speed to have.

Like most of the graveled county roads in the summer time, it was a dry and dusty road. The slightest wind or any vehicle going over it kicked up dust. In the winter it was covered with snow and mud.

Because the grade was steep, it could be slick and hazardous to drive on. Most people living in this part of the county drove four-wheel drive trucks or jeep-style rigs, as did we. We had wenches on the front of some of our patrol vehicles to help in case we slid off or needed to help someone out of a ditch.

But we didn't want to slide off this road. It was a long way to the bottom. No one was sure we would receive any assistance from the commune. And it would be hours before anyone knew we were in trouble and several hours later before anyone could get there to help us.

Once a deputy went over the top of the last hill and started down into the valley they were on their own. As I moved on down the road, I stopped off at a wide spot just before dipping down into the valley. The hills within and surrounding the ranch were a deep and beautiful purple. You could see for miles, and much of what was seen belonged to the commune.

It was said this was the point where Sheela stopped on her first visit, taking in the vista and deciding right then this would be the place they would buy. I still had another five-plus miles of the very narrow steep and bumpy road to go before I reached the ranch buildings and what had become a town in the middle of nowhere. This was a ranch turned into a small city by a commune that had caused consternation throughout Wasco County, the State of Oregon, and indeed, had become the focus of many people worldwide.

As I stood looking over the property, I couldn't help but think that these people did not like me, did not vote for me, and wanted as little to do with me as possible. They used intimidation to get their way and were not above using questionable techniques to obtain their objectives.

I would soon be out of radio range and out of contact with my office and any support I might need. I wasn't all that worried. I figured they wouldn't try anything on the ranch that would bring them under even more scrutiny. A thought that later would be proven false, at least for some of the officials.

I had my own way of intimidation if I needed it. I am not a particularly brave man; I had just learned through the years to do what needed to be done. I am right at six feet tall, plus I wore Wellingtons or cowboy boots that added a couple of inches to my height, and I have a heavy built. I learned a long time ago that my build and my knowledge of the law accompanied with a confident manner would carry me far in enforcing the Law.

One of my first training officers, a man who commanded respect just by his presence, was a big help to me. He told me that unless it was absolutely necessary, go into any situation low-key. If you have confidence in yourself and your abilities you can oftentimes quiet down a problem just by being there. You can always amp up your response if needed, but often it wouldn't be needed. If you went in too strong, it was difficult to calm down the situation as the people involved get more defensive.

This doesn't hold true in all circumstances, of course. Sometimes you have to go in hard to protect someone, to break up fights and/or shout to be heard. But, for the most part, it had worked well in my patrol days and in my dealings with almost everyone I met.

It was important that I go by myself. This was to be a statement of professionalism and an olive branch, of sorts, made by me to this organization as well as a show of self-confidence. I would not be intimidated. They needed to know that I was the sheriff. I was not necessarily their adversary. If they wanted to, they could be friends as well as constituents, but at the same time, I was not afraid to walk among them alone.

I got back into the Blazer, radioed that I was going into the valley and would be out of radio contact for at least three hours. I headed over the rise and down the road, to a hostile environment, all alone and with no backup.

CHAPTER 7

This was different territory than what I was used to as a law enforcement officer, and I couldn't help but reflect on that difference. I came from a City Police Department. While it was small by many standards, it was progressive and well trained. It also covered only seven square miles. It made little difference where you were, you knew you had radio contact. There were also back up officers available within minutes, if not seconds, from where you were if you needed them. Not here. Here you were on your own.

As a police officer, I had handled many different calls in my career. I had started as a Reserve Officer for the city department and then joined as a regular police officer later. I had worked my way through the ranks to Commander. I was good at being a police officer and commanding officer. I represented my department, my chief and my city in a professional and positive manner.

I had handled complaints, arrests, and investigations. I had given talks to groups, taught in schools, worked with organizations, taken and given training, all as a representative of my department. But this was also different.

For the first time, I realized what that difference truly was. Now not only was I representing my department, I WAS the department. I was the elected sheriff and what I did and said had a much different connotation. Continuing down the road along the basalt cliffs and towering rock formations, I soon found myself driving along a very large lake. I had no idea it was there. After about half a mile I came to the dam that blocked the creek and formed the lake.

The Creek was called Big Muddy Creek, and they had built the earthen dam on the creek so they could use the water for irrigation and recreation. I thought they had followed all the laws and had in fact done a good job. The dam was easily forty feet high and probably two hundred feet wide with a road across the top. I have no idea how thick at the base it was, but it was substantial and obviously built to last.

On its face was the commune's emblem, two doves surrounded by a white circle. This was made of stones painted white. It stood out brightly from the brown dirt of the dam. Below the dam the valley opened up, and I could see wide spots with bus signs and several side roads going up into the ravines in between the hills. Looking up the roads, I could see some buildings. They looked to be apartments but were too far away to get a good look. I learned these were several 4-plexes.

As I pulled into the main part of the ranch, coming into the city limits, the road became paved and much wider. At the beginning of the city, on the right side of the road, was a large paved parking lot. Next to the driveway and alongside the road was another guard shack and at the back of the parking lot was a large building.

I later learned the building was their Visitor's Center and Chamber of Commerce building. I could see the Fire and Police Departments' building on the left side of the county road, just past the entrance to the parking lot.

I noted a couple of police cars. There were also a couple of passenger vehicles, Chryslers, parked in front. They were fleet vehicles, alike in every detail, but they were expensive cars.

I went inside and introduced myself to the Chief. I noted she was young, in her mid-twenties, and attractive. She was wearing a uniform that was identical to the security officers'. However, the material was better quality, as was the leather Sam Browne belt holding her police equipment.

I later learned that many of the security and police officers had their shoulder patches, which depicted their department, velcroed on. This was done so when they worked as a Police officer they could put the police patch of whichever department they represented that day: whether it was the ranch city – the City of Rajneesh or the city that used to be Antelope and was now the City of Rajneeshpuram. Or when they worked as a security guard, they would put that patch on. All three patches were round in shape, of similar style, but different in wording.

The Chief appeared nervous, insecure and unsure of herself. She invited me into a side room where another young lady was seated at a table. She introduced herself. She was also in uniform and said she was one of the reserve officers. I found that very interesting. While reserves were respected by most officers, they were volunteers and could not be certified as police officers.

Their duties were different from department to department but usually consisted of tasks such as traffic control at functions, backing up the regular officers they rode with, security at public functions, security at crime scenes, and other "mundane" tasks that freed up the regulars to do the actual law enforcement duties.

Most worked a few hours a month. Many had undergone some training, and some departments had excellent training academies for reserves. They were not, however, full-time sworn officers. They had only limited authority within a department, and they were never policy makers.

They usually patrolled with regular sworn officers. While in uniform working for the department, as opposed to being away from the department, they had the full authority of a police officer within that jurisdiction. In the state of Oregon a sworn Police Officer, on or off duty, was a Police Officer wherever they went. That was not true of a Reserve Officer.

When chiefs and sheriffs met to discuss their departments you rarely found any but command officers, present, certainly not line officers. You never found reserves. Never. Yet, here she sat. I was curious. I could think of only one reason why she would be there: she was the one who was actually in charge.

Looking around I also noted that the mayor was not in the room. I wondered if he was listening to our conversation. The commune was very suspicious of me and my motives. While I had not campaigned to drive them out, I had defeated a man they knew. Some of the citizens who had supported and voted for me had made no secret of the fact they wanted to see the commune driven out of the county. The commune leaders were not happy with me.

They were wary of my motives and my real reason for being down there this day. I know they didn't believe that I was there just to shoot the breeze with another cop, but that really was the reason. The distrust and distaste were reflected in the demeanor of the two officers and in the tension, I felt in the room.

The leaders and I had already come to head over the security of the area during the festival. They were told by the County Court that they had to agree to the requirements. They had not been pleased with the list, and they were not happy when they complied. I was sure that had added to my cold reception. That was later confirmed in the demeanor of Mayor K.D. when he showed himself.

Another reason for the cool reception sprung from another problem the city faced. The State of Oregon Attorney General's office challenged their existence as a legitimate city. The Rajneesh were no longer allowed to send their police officers to the State-run Police Academy. This led to a show of militant force to the media, but that only further hurt their case. Their new officers could not be certified.

It was no secret that I was a strong supporter of the Attorney General and the Board on Police Standards and Training. That may have been one more point they were unhappy with me about. Still, I felt I was in my element. I was meeting with another police officer and of course the Mayor and, it would seem, with a reserve. I was the Sheriff, the Chief Law Enforcement Officer of the County, and I had earned my expectation of respect from the citizens. I knew it would take time, but I was confident that eventually, they would come to understand that I was a fair person. While I was not naïve, I also wasn't dealing with reality.

While the Chief had gone to and graduated from the Oregon Police Academy, she really didn't have much contact with officers from other departments. It became quite evident that she had very little experience. The reserve had no contact with officers outside their commune and no real interest in law enforcement.

I tried to find some common ground. I was told there was none. There was no crime on the ranch or in the city. It was a crime free city. They were Peace Officers, not Police Officers. They were there to protect the citizens from people on the outside that might come into the area and commit crimes. Crimes that would never be committed by their members. This was a mantra I was to hear a multitude of times over the next few months.

I asked questions of the Chief. I was genuinely there to learn about the department and the Chief. How large was her department? What type of ongoing training do they have? Normal questions between police officers.

However, the reserve would answer my questions. The Chief would either just agree or add a minor note or two when the reserve was finished. I turned my back on the reserve and pointedly asked the Chief some questions about her background. The reserve couldn't help herself, and she had to answer. This confirmed what I had first supposed when I had tried to set up the meetings and when I entered the room. She was a figurehead in charge of the department in name only. She had very little or no authority over the police department.

I liked the Chief. She seemed to be a nice person, but she was not a law enforcement officer either by nature or demeanor. With training in a real Police Department, she might have been a decent officer, but she wasn't at that time. My gut reaction would prove true in the fall when we started our investigation of a number of the Rajneesh leaders.

After I had talked for a while with the "officers," the mayor came into the room from a back room with a flourish, sitting down at the table. As I had surmised, he had been somewhere in the building watching and listening to what was being said. I figured he was just waiting, trying to get a handle on my methods, etc. before he came into the room. He came on the attack immediately. He said I was a politician elected by people who wanted his people driven out of the county.

Yes, there were a few that felt that way, I replied, and many citizens of the county had grown to distrust the commune and their methods. However, most didn't care if they were here or not, they just wanted to ensure they obeyed the law.

I told him I had been elected because I had a solid reputation as an officer for fairness and firm enforcement and I had excellent management and administrative skills. I told him that I was a Police Officer first and foremost, and I knew and enforced the law.

I went on to tell him that if it was necessary, I would stand between the commune and the other citizens of the county to ensure the commune's rights were protected. I would enforce the law no matter who chose to break it. We sparred back and forth over that and some more issues. As I said, he did not trust me. Of course, I didn't trust him either.

It was obvious to me he considered me a politician throwing sand on the skids of their operation. I was to be treated with contempt while I treated him with respect. My gut didn't care for the man. He was an egotistical jerk. I had the heartburn to prove it.

While I was rather enjoying the give and take it finally occurred to him that we were not going to get anywhere with the discussion. In disgust, he asked me if I wanted a tour of the city. The Mayor wanted to show me the city so he could show me how they set up the ranch for the 15,000 visitors coming into the ranch and city area during the festival.

I said I would love to have a tour.

CHAPTER 8

We then got into one of the passenger vehicles and we drove north, farther into the city. During the entire tour, we did not get off the county road, nor did we get out of the car.

However, most of the city and buildings were adjacent to the road. There were several apartment complexes and four-plexes up the side roads, and a complex of manufactured houses just past the ranch house. These were neighborhoods, much as you would see in any city.

The difference was they all belonged to the commune and were on private roads. Their meeting auditorium and a hotel was on another paved road off the county road, but could be seen about half a mile away.

I knew many of these buildings were in a contested battle over whether they should be allowed to stand. The county had not issued permits for them, and the Commune had taken it to court. It was a bitter dispute. I didn't say anything about it. It wasn't in my jurisdictional duties, and I sure didn't want to say something that might come back later to haunt the county. I did think about it, though.

On the east side of the county road was their airport. The runway was a mile long and over fifty yards wide. They had a small terminal across the way. Parked on the side of the runway on its own tarmac next to the terminal was a Convair 240 twin engine passenger plane, about the size of a B17, the commune owned.

Getting onto the airstrip was a complicated process. One had to have permission from the Rajneesh. But it was also tricky landing, I am told. Because it was between high ridges, the wind impacted the landing procedure.

They had several planes, most of which were smaller in size. I noted there were a number of prefabricated buildings along a private paved road that ran parallel to the runway on the east side of the runway. These buildings consisted of a hanger, plus a number of maintenance and storage areas.

I had been told by my campaign manager (who had visited there in the past) there was also a regular television studio in the upstairs of one of the buildings. I didn't ask about it.

Closer to the main part of the city at the end of the runway, and on the east side of the road, were several paved lanes about 20 feet wide and 60 or so feet long, with about two or three covered benches alongside each lane. I learned these were bus pick up points to be used during the festival.

They had regular bus stops throughout the ranch and regular routes to pick up the followers and then take them back to that location. They would then walk up to their rooms. There were two lakes that were on the property that were used for recreation and they, too, were on the route.

There was also a bank of about 20 pay phones on the east side of the bus lanes. Along the west side of the road, was a large lot full of yellow school buses. While I didn't count them, there appeared to be well over 50 of them.

There were several small fields where they would be setting up the temporary shelters. Those shelters consisted of canvas tents on wooden platforms. They would house four people each. This was to be the fourth year they had the festival. They would have those shelters up and ready in just about 3 days from start to finish.

They were well organized and had a lot of members to accomplish the work. Many of the apartments and four-plexes had been built to house visitors during the summer months and festival time. They remained empty the rest of the year.

We drove over a small bridge crossing the Big Muddy Creek. On the left, as we turned the corner to the right, still on the county road, was the old ranch house and some operational buildings. Now they were offices and a bakery for the commune. We drove south into the business district.

The business district was about a normal city-block long. It filled up the west side of the road. The main structure resembled a two-story mall. There was a covered wooden sidewalk all along the front of the stores. The stores consisted of a travel agency, beauty shop, gift shop, restaurant and a couple of other convenient stores. Most of the upper level was a large open office complex. The corporate offices were located in this area.

The rest of the upstairs was another restaurant. As we passed the stores, we went to the bookstore. It was in a separate building on the east side of the street.

We then drove by a number of four-plexes. Like those up the numerous draws, these were permanent buildings, built on a foundation and complying with all building codes, but without planning commission approval.

Beyond those buildings were other buildings I was told were classrooms for the Rajneesh's college and for seminars that were held throughout the summer. We passed this area, and I could see a large vacant field and then an opened covered area of about 40,000 square feet.

The vacant field of a couple acres would house more temporary shelters. We stopped at the covered shelter for a moment. There were no walls, just pillars holding up the roof. He explained that this was a field/mobile kitchen area, and the main dining area.

There were a number of prefabricated buildings on the north side of the shelter. These were used for storage of food during the festival. The floor was of concrete, and there were a few picnic tables. He told me that there would be hundreds of tables set up for the festival. Past this area was a very large space they use for recreational activity such as soccer. Still driving south we drove across the county line into Jefferson County.

There was another large field and a set of buildings about a half-mile down the road. He explained that this area was used for recreation, soccer, softball and other games.

We drove around to the buildings. I noticed two ambulances and was informed this was their medical clinic. He told me that it had examining rooms and an emergency room. I thought that was strange. Every other building was in Wasco County, why would they have their medical clinic in Jefferson County, so far away from the rest of the buildings? The answer became apparent to me in July during the festival.

As we turned around, he pointed to a paved road coming from the north, crossing the county road and leading away from the county road towards the south part of the ranch. He mentioned that the paving equipment was down this path to the south, but did not drive there. I knew that this was the road the Bhagwan Rajneesh drove on. There were pictures taken here of him going down the row of his followers as they lay flowers on the hood of his car.

The road was built after he got a couple of citations for driving without a license. Hitting a concrete truck head on didn't help matters. He lacked in the driving skills department. Since he liked to drive, the commune built this road for him. It was about twenty miles long and, except for crossing the county road, it was all on their private property.

The Mayor drove me back to the police building. As I got out, he asked me if I would approve the festival permit now. I told him I still had some concerns, and they had not met all the conditions I had put down for it to be approved. When he did that, I would review them and then I would get back to him. He drove off in disgust. I headed back to the office.

Almost four hours after radioing I would be going into the valley,

I was back on top radioing my return to service. I did remember to thank God for his guidance and calming hand. I was pleased by my exchange at the commune, but I knew they would be analyzing their tapes and every minute I was on the property. Who knew what they might think they found?

On the way back, I stopped in at the ghost town of Shaniko, population twenty, about forty miles from the ranch. I had lunch at the Shaniko Hotel and met the new owners.

They were great people. He was a retired plumber from Salem, Oregon. They had done a lot of work on the hotel, which had been built in the late 19th century and had been allowed to deteriorate to the point of uninhabitable. They were changing that fact. He took me for a tour. The rooms were on the second floor. Rather than numbers, he used names of local families. It was a welcome change after my visit with the Rajneesh.

Before he came, there was just one bathroom to be used by the tenants. He had placed a bath in each room. They had created a honeymoon suite with a Jacuzzi bath and upscale fixtures. They had cleaned up the foyer area and the outside of the building. They wanted to make it a destination hotel for those people that wanted to get away from the hubbub of life and relax a bit.

They had a restaurant and had brought in an upscale chef. They managed to last a few years, but their age and health worked against them. When you lived in what was basically a ghost town, your choices for employees was limited. While they had the hotel, they went through several chefs and had to depend on employees from either Madras, about 40 miles away or Maupin, about 30 miles away. Both of these communities were small and that also capped his abilities to get reliable help.

Even though people were quite used to driving several dozen miles in that country, it was expensive. They could get better jobs closer to home. He had steady clientele from around the area but, again, it was limited to people close by and it was not a very populated region. It wasn't enough to sustain the business and eventually he had to close the restaurant. After a satisfying meal, I headed back up to the office.

This trip was to be the first of many trips to the ranch. At that time, I had no idea that it was to be one of the busiest in the Wasco County Sheriff's Office history, and indeed, there would be one of the largest interagency investigations that up to that time had ever been held in the State of Oregon.

My first year was only two and a half months old. I had many things on my priority list. I knew there was a problem with two people in key positions. They were both nice guys, but they operated in a 1950's and 1960's mentality. Their techniques left something to be desired. The world of law enforcement had changed through the years. Too many of the deputies had not.

The Sheriff's Office was different than the Police Department. I "knew" that, but in practice it takes patience. The sheriff was elected and directly responsible to the citizens. A Police Chief has several layers between him and the public. Not to say a Chief's job was easier, the two were just different and require a different approach to the citizenry.

That was true of most of the County positions that were in Wasco County at the time. All of the positions were elected to office. The offices included the County Clerk, County Treasurer, County Assessor, County Surveyor, who also was County Road Master by order of the County Commissioners, County Judge, Commissioners that were similar to the city council, and County Sheriff. They were directly responsible to the citizens, period.

The first thing I noticed and appreciated was the closeness of the County officials to the citizens. They were willing to respond to the needs of the citizens and help them do what they needed to do. The Planning Director was appointed by the Commissioners and answered directly to the County Judge. While we would see City Planners just say no to projects, the attitude of the County planner was to try and see if they could help them do the project legally.

The County Road Department had the same basic responsibility to citizens outside the city as the city street departments had inside. There were over 900 miles of roads in the county, about 70 miles inside the City of The Dalles. The other incorporated cities had one, maybe two miles of streets.

Wasco County was nearly three thousand square miles. The Dalles had a little over seven of those. At the time, half the population lived within the City of The Dalles, with about half of the rest of the population within just a few miles. The rest of the population was anywhere from 10 to 100 miles away.

We had four small cities that did not have a Police Department, so we performed the duties in those communities as well as the several miles in between and all around. Antelope (Rajneeshpuram) and the City of Rajneesh had their own Peace Department, but the only ones happy about that were the Rajneesh. The rest of the citizens called us. For the most part, those areas were being serviced adequately. We needed to do a better job, but I had other responsibilities within the Office where I needed to focus most of my energy.

My Chief Deputy, again a great guy, should never have been appointed to the position. His mindset was to be just one of the boys, and his management training and style was non-existent. He would have been okay as a deputy, but not in that position. My Corrections Chief, again a nice guy, was probably okay when they appointed him, but he, too, was not up to modern techniques and rules of conduct. He also considered the Jail "his" domain and resented any interference.

I had a dilemma. I had determined when I ran that I would give everyone a chance in their positions. I knew that many of these people had been in service to the county for several years. They had not been held to a more professional standard, and their training had been virtually non-existence after the basics.

There was a "personality" about the Office that made it acceptable to be lackadaisical about their duties and no real accountability. There was no goal or direction. It just went day by day, operate by the seat of your pants, and that was okay.

This was the way it had been run "forever," and no one thought to change it. Things were being done and said that had no place in a modern Law Enforcement agency, especially in today's litigious world. The County had suffered some serious financial difficulties in the recent past, and every Office had to cut back their expenses. The Sheriff's Office was no different.

One of the places that were cut back was training, but it had never really been a priority. The training budget, for about 35 employees, was $1000. It would take me several years to bring that up to a more acceptable level.

However, in Oregon, there was a lot of training where the cost to the agency was getting the deputy there (and of course losing the services of the deputy for that time). Everything else was furnished, without cost to the agency.

We had the Police Academy operated by The Board on Police Standards. The academy paid for the staff, instructors, housing and feeding of all students. It was funded by a specified portion of the fines levied by the courts against violators. These classes were important. Most dealt with the boots on the ground type training, but there was a lot of management training available.

Also, there were classes held in different communities throughout Oregon to enable classroom training to be less expensive since they were just a day or two in length and, again, the financial burden on the agency was just the time spent by the employee. Since the employee was either within his jurisdiction or close, they could respond to calls if necessary.

Wasco County had little involvement with these classes. In evaluating where I thought the best bang for the buck in getting the Office on a more professional track, I came to the conclusion I had to train the supervisors and managers first.

It worked for some. Some resented it, and for some it was ineffective. The second group fought me, and the third just couldn't do what was expected of them.

But I began the process of upgrading the Office. In retrospect, I would have given those that either couldn't do the job or those who fought me far less time than I did. I could only peripherally address things like the fact I found out that personnel files, located in the administrative part of the jail, and were open to all. Anyone could view them: a direct violation of several laws.

CHAPTER 9

relocated the files as soon as I could put a lock on them. When a crime was investigated, reports were written. Several cases were placed in just one file, whether open cases or closed, making it difficult to locate and opened us up to some disclosure problems. If a lawyer asked for a file he could have access to several cases, none relating to his client, but might expose other things. That was changed.

There were several other administrative issues that had to be addressed in between everything else. The most complaints I had against a department within the Office was Animal Control, and sometimes the lack thereof. No one actually had oversight of the department, and I foolishly took it on instead of delegating it. However, in my defense (kinda, although I recognize I am a control freak), the sergeants didn't have the time, and I quickly realized the Undersheriff was struggling with having to do more than shuffle papers. I couldn't trust him to do even this task.

My time was divided. I was spending 60 to 80 hours a week, sometimes driving for several hours in addition to meetings, on the 9-1-1 issue, so I was out of the office just trying to juggle everything. Especially the jail issue.

The Jail became my biggest concern. Not only because there were serious issues in the operation, but also some of the equipment: the stove had been giving problems for the cook, and management had just waved it off without getting it fixed, for example.

It was a major concern because it was gas and had already malfunctioned and burned one of the trustees assigned to the kitchen. The stove was one of the first things I had repaired when I took office.

It was an old jail by Oregon standards (I have met sheriffs from the east coast using jails that were a hundred and more years older than ours). In the center of a large room was a US Navy brig, placed there when the Courthouse was built in 1914. It was antiquated, to say the least.

The bull pen's brig had ten one-person cells in the center of the room. It was designed to be four-person cells, but on advice from the Corrections Division it had been reduced to one per cell, and the other bunks were removed. The cells were about eight feet by six feet.

There were two rows, back to back, of five cells each, with a shower at the far end. Across from those cells was a single cell that used to be called the "rubber room" where inmates with psychiatric problems had been housed. Unlike the other cells, there was no toilet facility. It had not been used for that purpose for several years.

The soft material was removed from the cell, so it had bare walls. Inmates would be placed here for disciplinary measures. It was kind of an isolation room, ideally for just a day or two since there was a steel door that cut the inmate off from everyone except the CO, who checked in on him every hour.

In the hallway, leading from the main jail door to the door opening up onto the bullpen there was an individual, maximum security cell used for more violent or high-risk inmates. We also had a couple of two-inmate cells that we mainly used for trustees: inmates who worked around the courthouse and were given extra credit on their sentence.

We had one cell reserved for females, which was away from the general population. A door accessed it in the administrative office. Part of the complex, but out of sight and hearing of adult inmates as required by law, was a four cell Juvenile detention facility that also had to be cared for by the CO.

During this first year, I had all male Corrections Officers (COs). The clerical staff, all female, would book in any female prisoners and would see to their needs. The COs related well with the inmates.

There was only one CO on duty in most instances. They were by themselves in the jail with only the clerk/dispatcher, watching cameras, as their protection. If the clerks were too busy, the CO was in danger. They did not carry radios, so if attacked they were in trouble. They could not depend on immediate help from the deputies because they could be on patrol several miles away. It was just them. They had to deal with anything that came up, alone. The inmates knew, and some took advantage. For the most part, the inmates were people from the community, and many of them had been "guests" several times. It was like old home week when we brought some of them in. Few had a history of violent crimes in the county, most of these men did not pose a danger to the lone officer on duty. These were placed in the bullpen and used those cells. Sadly, on several occasions fights would break out where deputies and city officers had to come in to assist.

Oregon Law required that inmates could go no longer than 14 hours between meals. To ensure as much as possible the officers would be safe, meals were served at shift change in the morning, 0700, and afternoon, 1600, so two COs were there. We also furnished a snack, usually popcorn, later in the evening to be sure we complied with that law. At about 1800 hours the inmates went from the more open bullpen to the brig/cells where they were confined to a narrow, barred hallway.

Oregon law required an inspection by the Grand Jury once a year. There were no problems listed. In fact, the comment was often made about how clean the facility appeared. Cleaning was done by the trustees. But these were civilians, quickly passing through and not understanding what they were looking at.

We were not a "bad" jail. We treated our inmates with respect. When we eventually got sued, the lawyer told me the inmates had asked him what would happen to the jailers when he told them he was going to "shut us down." He had never been asked that question before. When we did shakedowns, we rarely found weapons. The inmates felt safe enough that they didn't think they had to defend themselves. Our fast turnover probably helped in this matter.

What we would find was a few food items, such as fruit or extra milk in cartons. We would also occasionally find "pruno": a crude alcoholic drink made of fruit and sugar fermenting in a bit of water. All were considered contraband and violations.

We did have television, some books, and board games and that was about it for distractive activities; we needed something to keep inmates busy. And we had down-home cooking. We had a cook that prepared meals for all inmates, juveniles, and the staff.

The inmates were in the jail 24 hours a day, seven days a week. Dissatisfaction with anything, even minor issues, could work on their minds. Food quality was one of the major complaints of inmates. No one ever complained about the quality or quantity of Wasco County meals. Our cook did a good job.

She would prepare meals for the weekends and place them in the refrigerator for trustees or COs to throw in the oven and then serve. No oven meant no food. So the fact that it remained unreliable was a major problem.

Upon taking Office, I found out that the Wasco County Jail was on an attorney's hit list. He had successfully sued some older jails, such as ours, in the state. Wasco County had a target on its jail, he but needed an inmate to complain to him. And word traveled fast when you were a prisoner in the State Prison system.

In addition to the Grand Jury, jails were to be inspected each year by the Corrections Division of Oregon. Our jail passed each inspection. But as I was to find out, that was more of a rubber stamp than a real evaluation that would encourage changes that could have prevented us from being sued, or at least limit our vulnerability.

What bothered me was even though several jails had been successfully sued, the Corrections Division Inspectors did not review them, or at least well enough, so they could help sheriffs who had jails that were being targeted.

For whatever reason, it appears my predecessors did not discuss those issues with the sheriffs that had been sued. While it wouldn't have made much difference in the outcome of our suit, it would have at least helped us be better prepared for it.

To help keep the jail from being sued, my predecessor had asked for advice from the State Corrections Division on how to change the jail to avoid a suit. They came and drew up a plan that would help improve the facility, and hopefully, either keep us from or allow us to win in a lawsuit.

Some of the work had been done. Downsizing the cells was one of them. The majority of the changes, though, had not been started. The main reason was the expense. Finances were tight, but it should have been a priority for the previous Sheriff and therefore the County. It wasn't. The Commissioners had a lot on their plate with the Rajneesh. This was not critical to them.

I do feel sorry for my predecessor. He wasn't experienced in either law enforcement or public administration. This was another area he was lied to. Others under his command remained incompetent. He had a lot working against him. But even with that he let many things slide, obvious things, that he could have resolved and didn't. He didn't address issues he should have and I, along with others I appointed into key positions, had no choice but to fight through the animosity and reluctance of change to get it done.

Because the jail could not hold everyone that was arrested, on the advice of the auditor, they had also instituted a point system, borrowing the system from other agencies and adapting it to Wasco County. Each inmate was judged on several criteria. If the points were low, they were often released on their own recognizance (RO). Or, if the incoming inmates were more dangerous than ones already housed, the older inmates would be released. It was a frustration. I had come from being a police officer that threw people in jail, to having to approve which one(s) was to be released on a daily basis. Jail meant nothing to these people.

On the surface, it appeared that the jail was okay, but I saw issues, like the stove, which were not being addressed and were not okay and even dangerous. As I inquired about things, I found that the Corrections Manager stonewalled me however he could. If I didn't ask something, he didn't tell me. He was withholding critical information from me. I couldn't prove it at first, and I wasn't familiar enough with a jail to know the questions to ask.

During that first year, to help me figure out what I needed to do in both the operation of the facility and keeping from being sued, I visited several jails, both older and newer and those sued and not sued. This took up even more of my time. I talked with the sheriffs and their corrections managers, trying to gain insight into what we could do to improve our jail operations.

I also took a two-week CO class, offered by the Board early that spring, for certified police officers that were going to be transferred to the jails within the state. Many sheriffs had to cut back on road personnel and in the process of seniority, would put them in the jails, replacing COs with less time. These had to be certified within a year. I resented doing it. Still, it had to be done because I couldn't depend on my manager. I was needed at the Office. I didn't like having to manage from two and a half hours away, taking two or three daily reports from two managers I couldn't trust to uphold my policies.

Sometime during that two-week class, in the middle of the day, an incident occurred in the south part of the county. Although it was serious, I can't recall just what it was. I do recall contacting the airport close by to the academy and ascertaining if they could fly me to the nearest location, which would have been in Madras. There I would have had one of my staff pick me up.

I was told they could do so and have me on my way within just a few minutes if need be. It was serious enough that everyone in the class knew about it; I think it was on the news. Whatever it was resolved quickly and I didn't have to leave. One of the COs in the class said that would have been a long drive. Before I could respond, the instructor laughed and said, "Sheriffs charter planes in those situations." He hadn't heard me, but of course, he was right. Just an aside I found interesting.

Going to the class and visiting jails, talking to sheriffs and Corrections Managers did assist me in understanding Corrections laws and how they applied to jails. I picked up several ideas that would help us upgrade the operation, as well as being able to ask more pointed questions of my manager. All of this was necessary because of the lax management and bad promotions I inherited with the office.

I learned a lot from the Oregon Academy classes but had a lot of problems with one of the instructors. He was the lead attorney from the State Attorney General's Office for the State prison system. He would go into the laws concerning incarceration and the application. What I didn't appreciate was his comments to COs about not letting their sheriffs kowtow to the attorney that was going around the state suing them.

I found out he did this in every class he taught, berating those that had done so. First, he had no business undermining the sheriff, especially since he was talking to COs who had no say in policy. Most were brand new recruits. Second, most jails housed some pre-trial inmates. They couldn't make bail, so they sat in jail. The standards for a pre-trial inmate and a convicted inmate were different.

The rights of the two types were different. Since the convicted inmate in jail was a misdemeanant, they were treated the same as pre-trial. There isn't enough room in any jail to keep the two separated.

In the prison system, it was different. They were all convicted. A prison inmate doesn't have the rights of a pre-trial inmate who was presumed innocent. This instructor was teaching County CO, not prison CO, but teaching as if they had the same requirements for the inmates. We had a bit of discussion about that, yet he was still used, and some sheriffs thought highly of him. They knew I didn't and would sometimes rib me about it. I told them this guy wasn't teaching in our best interest, and he just didn't "feel" right. So much for a gut instinct.

It wasn't too long before he left Oregon for another State to become a warden in one of their prisons. It was a while after that, though, that it was discovered he had committed felony crimes in Oregon and was disgraced. I got a few "guess you were right" comments from the sheriffs.

Back to the facility. I took what I had learned and the recommendations about changes to the jail seriously. The jail was taking up too much of my time, but I had no choice. I had a better understanding of what was going on and could catch my manager on misleading information. He was reluctant to institute some of my changes and sometimes said he did but hadn't. He resented being told what to do in "his" domain.

One of the things the Corrections Manager did that irritated me was his order to the clerks and COs to call him before anybody else, and he would come down to evaluate the situation and decide if anyone needed to be advised. While most of the calls were mundane, there was more than one that was serious and the patrol sergeant should have been told immediately. Failure to follow the order would get them on his "list," and he would make them pay one way or the other.

When that finally came to my attention, I ordered that the on-duty sergeant would be advised, and he would decide if the manager or I needed to be contacted. The manager was not happy.

We were in my Office when I told him what was going to be done, and reaffirmed that I wanted him to be more open with me. He said, "My responsibility begins at that door," pointing back towards the jail area. I said, "My responsibility begins at the front door and includes all of it!"

He got the message. However, he still undermined me whenever he could. We had weekly staff meetings where the sergeants and the manager could bring up things and help turn the Office around. COs would ask him to bring things up, but he didn't. After a while, I learned that he would go back and tell them that the sergeants cut them down, and the Sheriff said no. Talking about undermining the rest of management and the morale of the COs. They had some good ideas once they were presented. It took a while, but he was eventually terminated.

During my first meeting with the County Budget Committee, I reviewed what was happening with the lawsuits across the state. I had not digested all of what I had and would learn as I continued to talk to the other sheriffs, at least we had a plan of action. An expensive one, but it needed to be done. I took the recommendations from the advisor and a five-year plan to address those recommendations. They were prioritized so the most important could be done first. They signed off on the plan.

As I did more research and looked at our facility, it became apparent that there would be things that we couldn't overcome. What we hoped for was that what we were doing would be enough to hold off until we could get a new jail built.

I told the County Judge that if we were sued, we would not fight the suit, but try to work with the attorney. In a lawsuit of this kind, if any part of the complaint was upheld then the Federal Judge could award attorney fees and other fees up to three times the amount requested. We could not afford to run that risk.

When we were sued. They filed a brief. I reviewed them and thought that we could negotiate a lot of it out, because some of it conflicted with the plan the Advisor from the Corrections Division had given us. I sent the suit to him and asked him to come to the jail. A few days later he came and inspected the jail. He said that the changes requested by the attorney were good ideas.

In the plan, we were to spend a great deal of money making changes that the attorney was opposed to. If we had made those changes, then it would have been for naught. Even some of those that were made by my predecessor had to be scrapped. I challenged him about his prior inspections and the plan he had devised for us. He said something like, "The inspections were not meant to make it hard on Counties, especially smaller ones like yours." So his inspections were just scans. The jail was clean, inmates well fed, so he didn't see any point in putting the jail down. While that was "nice," it proved detrimental. I was less than happy.

We started to negotiate with the attorney. In the process, we ended up making our jail a "72-hour holding facility" so it didn't have to follow all the guidelines and requirements the attorney was trying to put through. We no longer had a jail, just a short-term facility. Part of our salvation was we were able to negotiate that an inmate could sign a waiver and remain in our facility for a longer term than 72 hours; for them, it was a jail.

For those that thought they could wrangle a get out of jail card by not signing, and were too dangerous or otherwise scored too high of a point, we took them to another jail adjoining our county. That was an important fact. Oregon law allowed a sheriff to hold a pre-trial inmate in a jail of an adjoining county. We had several to choose from: Hood River County in Hood River; Clackamas County in Oregon City; Marion County in Salem; Lynn County in Albany; Jefferson County in Madras; Wheeler County in Fossil, which didn't have a jail, so they housed some of their prisoners with us and other adjoining counties; Sherman County in Moro, which also housed their prisoners with us; and across the river in Klickitat County in Goldendale, WA (the law did not specify that we couldn't take them out of state. As long as the county was adjoining it could be done, and was being done by some Oregon sheriffs).

Some of those couldn't have helped us. Most were just too far away in both distance and driving time. We did have some options, and once the word got out, we had few who refused to sign the waiver. As I said, we treated our inmates with respect and they were near their relatives.

We signed a long-term contract for beds with Union County in La Grande, where we sent convicted misdemeanants. They were about 200 miles away and not adjoining, but didn't have to be when the inmate was convicted. They had been sued by the same attorney and were in compliance, so we knew that our prisoners couldn't sue Union County.

I knew from the beginning that we needed a new facility and had started planning on how we could get a bond levy through the citizens of our county to build one.

While that first year, with the hundreds of extra hours dealing with the problems, including personnel, in the jail was a real challenge for me, it continued to be an issue and a burden I had to deal with my entire time in Office. It required untold thousands of hours I would have preferred and needed to be doing something else.

CHAPTER 10

As spring went on we had to divide our attention to other duties of the Office with an only cursory overview of the Rajneesh. Their population enlarged as the weather changed. For the most part, it remained uneventful. Our deputies served papers without interference. As the weeks went on, though, we did have some unusual situations arise. The Rajneesh had people at all the County Commission meetings. That wasn't a problem, but it did put a damper on one thing.

At the first meeting of the month, the Department Heads were invited in to give a brief overview of what happened in their agencies. I looked forward to this when I heard about it. I wanted to hear how things were going with them and what they were doing as I just didn't know all the intricacies of County Government.

That first meeting I brought in a list of the things we were doing in the Office, trends in crime, etc. What I heard, from the others, though, were things like "everything was normal," "just the same things going on," "nothing new," and so on. The presence of the Rajneesh hampered our open communication. Not because we were trying to hide anything, but they would challenge some of the decisions and make a nuisance of themselves.

Someone came up with the idea of a monthly meeting of the Department Heads and only one commissioner. It wasn't open to the public because there was not a quorum of Commissioners. It was just information, not decision making, between departments. It was a relaxed and enjoyable experience. We were able to hear what was happening with each office or department, and we were able to assist each other when we had issues or things that were bothering us.

The meetings were not mandatory. When the Department Head wasn't available, he/she would send the second in command or just not be represented. As a result, I learned a lot about the county's operation. I appreciated the cooperation between the departments and the affirmation of everyone's desire to do the best they could for the citizens.

One of the county committees I was on as sheriff was the Wage and Classification Committee. It was assigned the task of reviewing job descriptions and determining what pay scale they should be assigned. I can't remember how many of us were on the committee, I want to say somewhere around eight department heads total. Several years before my election, the county had requested a review by a consultant of all jobs in the county to make a job description on each task and assign a wage scale. The county then received the formulas to help decide through this committee how any new jobs were to be evaluated and given a pay scale.

Like any large employer, Wasco County had several positions that were similar in nature no matter what department the person worked in. There were also many jobs that were so dissimilar in nature that they required the committee to review and make decisions independently. In addition to this process, the employees had joined unions. The negotiated wages were the ones currently in effect. For those departments that did not have union representation, those wages of similar positions, for example, clerks, would prevail.

There were many things to consider: type of job, stress from the job, type of stress, what authority the employee in that position had in making decisions, education and training required, similar positions in other departments within the county, and more. A numerical value would be assigned to each of them. We would then go to a table that was pertinent to that position. Management positions were not judged the same as non-management positions and, because of the type of work we did, law enforcement was separate from others.

A Department Head could ask for a review of his department's wages, usually either because he had a new position that wasn't listed before, or he had assigned more duties to the position and believed it should be evaluated. After reading the description and listening to the department head's explanations, we would independently assign the values to the position and then discuss them. Very seldom were we off more than a point or two from each other. The method was scientific, but allowed for anomalies, and it was easily applied.

Once the position was evaluated, the information would be given to the County Commissioners to approve or disapprove. Sometimes the committee would recommend that the department removed that position, but that was rare. And not always was the department manager happy with the wage scale given to the post. However, I have to say that the formula worked well. I was amazed at how accurate we could be in our recommendations.

Most of the job descriptions for the Sheriff's Office were on par, except for the position of Corrections Manager. I could not believe what I read. The sole, the only, job duty listed, was that he knows where all the furnace equipment in the courthouse was and how to operate it. There was nothing about supervision, nothing about running a jail. He simply needed to know how the furnaces worked.

Based on this job description it was determined that the position had the same value as a road deputy. The COs had a wage scale slightly lower than the road deputies so he was making more than his employees, but not by much. More importantly, the pay was not adequate considering the responsibility of the position.

My position has always been that each employee was valuable to the department. Each position had a value to the agency and just because a person's salary was less than someone else's, it doesn't mean the latter was more important than the former. Each individual helps the department complete its mission, and each person deserves respect regardless of how much money they make. However, they should be justly compensated for what they do.

I was talking with a reporter one day about the jail. I don't recall how we came to talking about the position of Corrections Manager, but the reporter was downplaying his position. One of the comments made was he wasn't making the money a sergeant was and therefore was lesser to the sergeants. Part of the problem was the person in the position. He was not very well respected by anyone. Some of it was the wage scale, but most of it was the person himself.

However, it wasn't the person we were evaluating at that time, but what the position was expected to do. This post was a crucial place in not just the Sheriff's Office but for the county. If the jail wasn't operated correctly, the liability of the county was at stake.

The Corrections Manger's position was much more important than depicted. I started to re-write that description. I did it for basically two reasons. First, it wasn't even close to being accurate. Second, it was becoming increasingly evident to me I was going to have to have a new corrections manager, and I needed a fair salary, even for the person currently in the position, and to entice someone to apply for the post.

Other sheriffs were gracious enough to let me use their descriptions, which I modified to fit our facility. I excluded the part about the furnace. We had maintenance personnel that took care of that.

When I was finished, I brought it before the committee. With all things considered, the position should at least make as much as a road sergeant. But the board would draw its own conclusions.

Based on the formula, the committee placed a wage on the position that was equal to the road sergeants. There was one difference. It was a managerial position, not a supervisory position, so the position did not receive any overtime. Like the Sheriff and Chief Deputy, he worked until the job was done, even if it took several hours beyond the normal 40 hour work week.

Somewhere along the line after I had asked the Undersheriff/Chief Deputy to resign, I decided to have two Lieutenants instead of that position. There was an Administrative Lt. who watched over the jail, among other administrative duties; and an Operations Officer, who was in charge of the road deputies and investigations. For whatever reason, it wasn't accepted by the deputies and just didn't work out. After a time, I went back to the Undersheriff/Chief Deputy position and promoted the Administrative Lt. to Undersheriff.

He was outstanding. Where my skills were weak, his were strong, and we made an excellent team. Through successions of Corrections Managers, we were even more reliable as the three of us met on a weekly basis. A large part of the success of our Office, through the years, can be placed on this man's shoulders. He was a rock and became a good friend.

Meanwhile, my office was about to explode with action. A former follower of the Rajneesh had some accusations we needed to investigate. Allegations involving children.

CHAPTER 11

That same spring, a former member of the Rajneesh called us to report child abuse and neglect on an epic scale at the ranch. Among the accusations were the children shuffled off to a building to languish with little care, with nothing to give them in mental stimulation or teachings. The parents worked twelve hour days and rarely saw their children. Rajneesh treated the children as if they were in the way. This person was concerned about their welfare. The former member had left the commune over a year before the phone call. I was told, by whom I can't remember, that it was not unusual for people of a suppressive society, such as the Rajneesh's isolationism, to take a while to overcome their apprehensions and to speak out.

Child abuse or neglect was a serious accusation. We investigated those complaints. All of them. One of our investigators and a Children Services Department (CSD) worker drove down to the ranch to investigate the charges. This would be the first time the CSD investigator went to the ranch. She was apprehensive. She voiced her reservations as they drove down. The deputy assured her she would be okay and said, "Just don't drink the Kool-aid."

That comment was about the massive murder/suicide of the Jim Jones cult a few years earlier. Within a day or two of their visit, I received a letter from the Chief. The tone was "how dare we investigate anything on their ranch." They had a peace department that should have done it. She went on to state that they were a crime-free city, and no child neglect was going on. She was also upset by the reference to Kool-aid.

My response was that as Sheriff, I or any of my deputies may investigate any alleged crime within the county, whether inside city limits or not. There was also the fact that the State's Attorney General had advised the Police Academy not to accept Rajneesh "Peace Officers" into the academy. Her people weren't certified and her "Peace Department" had no credibility. I didn't mention it, figuring why to add fuel to the fire. Instead, I asked, "Who heard a deputy saying anything about Kool-aid and where did they hear it?"

She did not answer my question. It was possible the deputy may have said something at lunch in the restaurant. He couldn't remember, but if done it wasn't where anyone could or should hear it. We had long suspected that we were being monitored by the Rajneesh. We continued to be careful about what we said about them.

It was doubtful they could have heard anything while the deputy was in the car, although the super microphones being used by major networks that can pick up conversations from as far away as 500 feet may have been available. We later learned it was entirely possible the Rajneesh had bugged the area in which they had lunch. Among the things we discovered in our investigation later that year was that outsiders, particularly officials, were always placed at certain tables in the restaurant. These tables were indeed bugged and conversations recorded. Illegally, of course.

Within a few days of the investigation, I received a phone call from a man who reported being an attorney for the Rajneesh. He demanded copies of the reports. One of the first things you learned as a police officer was that no one gets reports about an on-going investigation except those agencies involved. In this case, it would be the District Attorney and CSD.

I told him it was a case under investigation, and I would not give him any report. He ranted and raved, advising me that I had "better talk to my attorney."

He even threatened a lawsuit. I said, "You are free to speak to the DA about the reports."

He slammed down the phone. I did advise the DA that the Rajneesh were trying to get copies of our reports. He laughed and said, "There's a way to squelch this harassment."

He went to the presiding judge, who ordered a gag order which prevented us from talking to anyone. A few days later this same "attorney" called back and asked if the reports were ready to be picked up. I once again told him that it was an ongoing investigation, and we would not be releasing anything.

I listened to his ranting and threats for a while before I said, "That's all right, you can do what you want, I am not giving you copies of the report. And oh, by the way, the judge has a gag order on this."

My words added emphasis to the fact he wasn't going to get anything at this time. He slammed down the phone. We never had a conversation again.

The investigation didn't come up with any viable victims, but we left the case open in case we got more proof of a crime(s) later. Frankly, I was enjoying my give and take with the Rajneesh. Thus far we had won in every situation.

The Rajneesh went on the back burner while I addressed another critical item on my agenda. But even this concerned the Rajneesh and would be a sore spot for all concerned.

By the end of 1985, all counties had to have a 9-1-1 plan turned into the State, ready to be implemented the next year. It had to be signed by every emergency provider in the county, and then some. Wasco County had barely gotten started. They had hired a consultant to assist in the planning process, but that was all. The city of The Dalles had been on the 9-1-1 system for several years, had a call center set up, and was in compliance. The rest of the county was not. There was political and planning work needed to get the entire county in agreement.

It was incumbent on me to be deeply involved in this process. I only had a couple of people who I could assign to the job, but they had too much on their plate already. Those that had time on their hands did so because they remained untrustworthy. That meant it fell to me. The 9-1-1 plan took several hundred hours of my time that first year. Not only did we have meetings at every volunteer fire agency, as I recall now about eight programs, but we also had to meet with all the City Councils in the county.

Some of the phone lines in the lower part of the county went into Jefferson County's system. So we had that county's committee to work with. The Warm Springs Indian Reservation was partly in Wasco County, and some of their lines also went into Jefferson County. So we had their Fire and Police Chief, as well as the Tribal Council, who had to sign off.

I had to meet with individuals in the volunteer departments, listen to their concerns, and assure them I understood. I worked to make sure the integrity and individuality of their units were not damaged by the agreement. Lots of meetings, lots of miles, and lots of time.

One obstacle to full compliance was how to work with the volunteer fire and ambulance services around the county, in addition to the Rajneesh situation.

As I said, the city of The Dalles had been in the 9-1-1 system for several years. They had a communications center manned with dispatchers 24 hours a day. The state had levied a phone tax for 9-1-1 centers several years before 1985. The money was to be used only for the 9-1-1 calls, equipment, and administrative duties of forming a plan.

The City had used all its 9-1-1 funding received on those two telephone exchanges. Each year they had applied it to the com center. The funding was insufficient to operate the center, so additional funds were used from the City's general funds to augment the dispatching of City Police, Fire and Ambulance services for the two numbers assigned to the city.

There were citizens outside the City that also used those numbers, so any calls from them of a law enforcement nature were relayed to the Sheriff's Office, which had its own dispatchers. The ambulance service operated by the City Fire Department handled calls in both the City and the outside areas. The city dispatched the fire departments.

There were two fire departments that the City dispatched for: the City's and Wasco Rural. Wasco Rural handled all calls outside the City limits in The Dalles' telephone exchange. They paid the City for their additional services.

In actuality, the two fire departments acted as one. For several years they had been housed in the City Hall fire hall and assisted each other on calls. The personnel belonged to one or the other of the departments. However, most of us couldn't tell the difference. The taxes paid for the Wasco Rural Fire Dept. went to the city, who managed all administrative duties for both departments. It was a mutually beneficial arrangement, at least at that time.

As per law, the County and other incorporated cities within the county had been placing their portions of the 9-1-1 money into interest-bearing accounts until it could be used for the planning and implementation of the county plan.

Part of that money was used to pay the consultant for his time and advice. He was also the person who was to be the spokesperson for the planning process. The problem was one of trust: the agencies and cities outside the City didn't trust the City's council or personnel. They were afraid they would lose control of their program, and the service calls would be delayed due to the 9-1-1 operators being unfamiliar with the county and their area in particular.

I had to be involved in the process. I was going to get the volunteers to sign off on the idea. After all, I had been elected by a very wide margin. I figured it would be easy. I figured wrong.

While I was their elected Sheriff, I had been a police officer for the City of The Dalles. They had to be convinced my loyalty now was to the whole county, not just The Dalles. I had to prove I was there to help them.

The people in the rural portions of Wasco County did not trust or like The Dalles. No one trusted the Rajneesh, and they too had to agree since they controlled two cities. We had to overcome all of this if we were to get it done.

There were a couple of people on The Dalles City Council that had made it plain to the rest of the county that The Dalles should be in charge, and the rest just sign off. There was even demand that all the fire departments in the county had to contribute money to the operation.

I was opposed to that. First, they wouldn't have that many calls, and second, except for The City of The Dalles Police and Fire Dept., Wasco Rural Fire Department and the Sheriff's Office, the emergency providers, both fire, and ambulance, were all volunteers. They had little funding, if any, and it wouldn't be fair to them. I thought it was stupid. So did the Commissioners.

We did have the benefit of a respected County Judge. He lived outside one of our smaller communities in another part of the county. He was supporting our work, but still, the nuts and bolts of the plan had to be decided by ALL the agencies affected, and everyone wanted to protect their programs.

It was a long process. I spent dozens of hours driving around the county, not to mention the hundreds of hours talking to both the individual organizations and key people in those organizations, listening to their concerns and ideas, and then to assuring them, they would be heard.

Somewhere along the line, someone suggested using the hospital's dispatching service since they were there 24 hours a day to call in staff. We quickly dissuaded that idea. There wasn't a cop or fireman who would have agreed to that. It would be like having a telephone operator dispatch us.

Dispatching for emergency departments would be much too involved. They would have to pass background tests, go through a lot of state-mandated training, not to mention calling a doctor and dealing with people in crisis requires a different kind of personality. It was a highly stressful and specialized profession.

From start to finish a major supporter of the countywide plan was The Dalles City Manager, Del Cesar. He had enough respect from his council to give him the authority to negotiate. His flexibility and insights, along with his influence with the City Council, made all the difference in getting the City to agree to the plan.

Fortunately, the City Manager agreed with me, and the two of us worked very hard to get the whole thing together. Every entity had to sign off on the plan. And each wanted to protect their program's integrity and keep from being under the thumb of The Dalles City Council. Both of us understood that.

I always had liked the City Manager while I worked for the City. Didn't always agree with him, and we had some heated discussions (which wasn't my place to have, but he didn't hold it against me), but I learned to appreciate him even more during this process. Without his hard work and reputation with the City Council, it wouldn't have gotten done. At least, not as smoothly.

However, those volunteer agencies outside the City questioned his loyalties to the program. He was hired by The Dalles to follow the orders of the Council. While he was a big supporter of a county system, I did most of the legwork with the volunteers by myself. No point in adding fuel to the fire. He had many other things on his plate.

One of the concerns was the City controlling the center. The City was the eight hundred pound gorilla. Almost half of the citizens lived in the City limits. Some on the City Council wanted control. Their justification was that since the City would be putting up most of the funding, and had the center already in place, the City should have the control. Those that felt that way were not quiet. It was a major obstacle to the forming of the plan and the acceptance by those outside the city. We compromised by forming a separate entity. The Board of Directors comprised of a City Representative; a County Government Representative; a Representative of the Rural Fire Protection Agency, which covered the area in the two phone exchanges for The Dalles; and one Representative, who would represent all the other entities in the county.

Each entity had an equal vote. This became another sticking point with the City, who felt they should have more weight to their vote. The City Manager smoothed that over.

As I mentioned earlier, the money received from the state 9-1-1 plans was insufficient to operate a center on any level. It had to be propped up with other funds. The funding was an additional burden for the plan.

When I first talked with the volunteer organizations, most of them thought they would be getting pagers and new radios from the funding. I had to convince them that it was not going to happen. There just wasn't enough money to purchase these items and build and operate the center. It took a while, but we finally got them to understand it wasn't feasible.

Where the center was going to go was also a big issue. The City had a Center, inside the City Fire Department's hall.

That was not an acceptable location for the volunteers. They were afraid of too much City influence being placed in the center if it remained there. We located an alternate site in the Phone Company's building. They had a large room that was perfect for the center.

We had just three more obstacles to overcome. How were the calls to the volunteer agencies to be handled? We remedied that by leaving the telephone trees for each organization in place. There was some liability in doing this. All 9-1-1 calls must be responded to. Some were concerned that if we left those phone trees in place, a call might be dropped.

A phone tree system was basically one number to be called for services. That number was forwarded to a volunteer. The person that answers that phone then calls two more volunteers. They each call two more volunteers, etc., and the emergency agency responded. It worked in a lot of areas. It had been working for the volunteers for as long as anyone could remember. They weren't going to stop responding now.

It took a while, and the City Manager was a great help in this to convince the City that the volunteers were serious about providing services in their area, often assisting others in nearby areas. They would not drop calls. Leaving the phone trees in place enabled the 9-1-1 dispatcher to patch the caller into the agency and then let that agency handle the calls as they always had.

It gave the added comfort to the volunteers that they still controlled their responses since much of a rural area life was geography spent more on a person's residence than the actual address. Calls like, "This is Joe I need an ambulance up here." They could talk to the caller and get the necessary information.

CHAPTER 12

The second of the three road blocks was funding. The City used their center to receive all calls for the fire and ambulances, as well as the police department. They would then dispatch whichever agency was needed and maintain radio contact with them.

They also handled all other phone calls for service, and radio calls from the three departments. Some outspoken members of the City Council felt the volunteer agencies should also pay into the center. The City Manager, other board members, and I pointed out that the volunteers had NO funding sources. They did not receive any taxes. They had bake sales and fundraisers just to get equipment and gas for their vehicles.

Basically, we said to leave them alone, and that thought prevailed. There was a discussion of making the 9-1-1 center a separate taxing entity, distinct from the rest of the governmental entities, but that didn't get any momentum.

I wanted the same dispatching services for my Office that the City's Police Dept. received. We had depended on our clerical personnel to dispatch our units for years. The problem with that was not only were they trying to listen for deputies who may need immediate assistance and responding to their requests, but they also had paperwork and served as receptionists for our Office. To then answer phones from citizens calling in, and attend to female inmates while watching the monitors when the COs were in the jail area with detainees was a bit much.

When the clerks were away, a CO had to operate the radio, which was not a proper use of manpower. Deputies were at risk, as well as COs and the inmates. The Wasco Rural Fire Department also wanted to continue having their units dispatched by the center.

In an attempt to allocate costs and shares of the operation, we calculated, as close as possible, the number of calls by each agency. As I recall, the following was decided. As we reviewed the calls each organization had and how they were dispatched, it was found that law enforcement comprised about ninety percent of the calls. When we factored in the calls for city service and those for the Sheriff's Office we determined that the city had/would have more calls into the dispatch center.

We divided that so the City would pay fifty percent and the County forty percent for law-enforcement related calls. The Dalles and Wasco Rural would pay an equal amount: five percent for the fire and ambulance costs. All entities paying into the system agreed to the formula with a review to be done each year. The Director of the Center would submit a budget to the 9-1-1 Board, and after review and making any changes they would approve the budget and pass it along to the three paying entities.

The City, the County for the Sheriff's Office, and Wasco Rural would then take this budget to their coresponding committees to get it approved. This was different from some other centers around the state where the actual calls were counted as they came in and the individual agency was then billed for each call. We preferred our method. There was far less paperwork, and the formula has pretty well stood up over the years. We now had only one more roadblock. It was the most difficult of all.

Our second to the last meeting of the principles of the 9-1-1 Center was held at the Rajneesh Ranch. It was not a pleasant meeting. It was intended to be the last one before acceptance by all entities. The consultant would draw it all up, and the two of us would go to each entity to get signatures.

The District Attorney for Jefferson County attended the meeting with a Federal Mediator from Seattle. The DA had requested assistance from the Federal mediation program to help resolve issues between the Rajneesh and the rest of the citizens. I had no idea that this was happening. I am not sure who did, as it seemed to be a surprise to all of us there. But it definitely put an interesting twist to things. I later learned he had been onboard for quite some time, mainly working with the state and federal agencies.

One of the people on the committee made a reference to the "guard shacks" on the road. He was rudely and abruptly informed those were not "guard shacks" but information booths. He was then given the standard lecture as to why they were there and how much better the Rajneesh operated things than anyone else.

It went downhill from there. Before the meeting, we had pretty much agreed on everything. When the state law was passed, there was a time limit on how the cities would handle 9-1-1 calls to their entities. All but two of our cities had agreed to work with Wasco County to come up with a plan to answer the calls at the Wasco County Center.

During that time frame, Shaniko and Antelope wanted their 9-1-1 calls to go to Jefferson County, and their councils had passed a resolution to that effect. Those exchanges, like The Dalles exchanges, were also used by citizens outside the city limits.

I didn't have a problem with that. Most of the calls from that area were ambulance related, and it would be quicker to get an ambulance there from Madras in Jefferson County, even though Maupin's ambulance was the one most used and was about equal distance.

The primary concern of the residents was that the Madras hospital was about twenty to thirty minutes away, and The Dalles hospital was well over an hour. It made them feel better to have the closer medical facility and an ambulance from that area. The Jefferson County Center would route all law enforcement and fire calls to us. The few seconds to do that wouldn't make a difference to our operation. We would have to pay them for any and all calls to their center, but the cost was negligible.

In a matter-of-fact tone, the Rajneesh declared that they no longer wanted the Antelope 9-1-1 calls to go to Madras since they had a 24-hour dispatching service at the ranch. They wanted the calls to go there. Of course, now they were in charge of the City of Antelope. They also had a city on the Ranch and both those cities, along with their Police and Fire Chiefs, had to approve of the plan. The mediator thought that was an excellent idea. I didn't. I also knew that if we didn't include their wishes we would lose.

I didn't discuss it with the other entities. I knew that I would not sign off on a plan that would allow the Rajneesh to decide if they wanted to let my Office know of any 9-1-1 calls. I also knew the citizens living inside AND outside Antelope's city limits would be placed at risk from Rajneesh shenanigans. Citizens already felt they had to watch their backs, knowing that somewhere lurking in the shadows there could be Rajneesh watching them. They hadn't forgotten the "presents" of animal feces, the lights shining into their homes late at night, or being watched for hours by Rajneesh. One incident reinforced their concerns.

The Rajneesh had several small planes for their use and, from what I understand, a couple of good pilots. One night, mid-spring, I received a call from the 9-1-1 system that a small aircraft had crashed just east of Antelope. It was believed to be one of the Rajneesh planes.

I decided I would go with my deputies, given all the problems we had in that area. The plane was flying at night. The pilot had misjudged where he was on the hill. He was a couple of feet too low when the plane hit the ridge. Pilot and passenger were flung out of the aircraft.

The first deputies on the scene were given some off-road vehicles by ranchers to use to drive to the crash scene. It was a mile or so out of town and very steep terrain. It was not known exactly how fast the plane was flying. We do know the aircraft flew into the hill at a high rate of speed. Two seater planes were flimsy and not made to withstand crashes, especially one like this.

The deputies arrived at the scene, which encompassed several square yards as the debris flew all over. The plane was demolished. It was not the only thing in pieces. The two people on the plane were also mangled beyond recognition. People were not made to withstand this kind of trauma.

One of the deputies obtained the wallet of the pilot, which contained his identification. They also found the identification of the passenger. We left a deputy at the scene until the FAA investigators could come in and do their job.

The next morning the remains of the two people were taken into The Dalles. While we were pretty sure these were the right names, we had learned that the Rajneesh were not always honest with us, so we had to take steps to get the best identification possible. Someone talked to the people at the airport. These people knew the two dead, confirming the names on the license. Dental records would be attained as well, but we felt we had enough information to contact the family.

One of the things we have been taught in death investigations was that it was best for the family if the family can view the body. It helps for identification, but also for closure. It can be tough for the family to mentally accept the death of their loved one. Not seeing the body can be problematic for them.

For many, it causes a great deal of mental anguish and pain if they can't get that closure. But there were exceptions. This was one of them. We met with the wife and a couple of other family members in our meeting room. The woman had been told by the mortician, that she should not see the remains. She had tentatively confirmed who he was by his ring, but she wanted to see her husband's body.

She wanted our help to get him to let her see her husband. Understanding the need for closure, I first was supportive of that viewing. Our sergeant knew that and kept giving me the high sign not to push it. As gently as possible, the sergeant told her that she should remember her husband as he had been. The body being unrecognizable. It took time, but she eventually accepted his advice.

We will never know why the pilot chose to fly to the ranch so late at night, well after sunset. We were told that he was their best pilot and knew the approach better than anyone else. This wasn't like flying into a major airport. Antelope only had a few houses, the lighting was negligible. The area he was flying into was like a black hole, no light at all.

The landing strip was surrounded by hills. The air currents and the narrow approach getting into the ranch were tricky. The pilot knew that. There were no landing lights to guide him onto the runway. When he hit the hill, it was at night. He could not see it. Since the airstrip was unlit, we were not sure how he could gauge the landing.

From everything we learned, he was a good pilot, dedicated and safe. How important was the trip to cause him to throw caution to the wind to get his passenger to the ranch? We weren't told. It didn't and still doesn't make sense that he flew to the ranch that night instead of waiting for the next morning. It was a tragic incident that just compounded the local peoples' concerns about what was happening in and around the ranch.

I am sure I was not the only member thinking I would refuse to sign off on letting the Rajneesh handle emergency calls. Because this was a new wrinkle everyone agreed that it would have to be discussed with each agency's board or governing body, and we would meet at a later date.

CHAPTER 13

At first, I wasn't sure how I was going to address this issue. On its surface, this appeared fine. But it wasn't the surface that concerned me. I knew that if we agreed to this, we were placing people at risk. People I had sworn to protect.

The summer of 1985 fire proved my fears. I had heard numerous times that a crisis can bring people who are usually at odds with each other together. That may be true in some instances. It was not true in this community. While the city lies between some hills, it also has several wheat ranches adjoining the city limits.

It was not unusual to have fires in those fields, and they move fast like a prairie fire. You have to get out in front of it before the winds sweep it too far out of control. A friend of mine, an Oregon State University Extension agent, was in the area at the time, so he quickly drove over to see if he could help. This story came from him.

This fire was coming from the north. The locals started making a fire break just outside the city. Since they didn't have construction equipment at the scene to do that, they had to use shovels. To do that you have to use a shovel like you were loading a furnace with coal scooping the dirt and throwing it.

The Rajneesh, however, had no idea how to combat a fire. What few were on the fire line were separated from the other citizens. Instead of scooping and throwing they were trying to dig into the dirt, lift it, and throw it. The agent showed them how to properly dig the line.

The Rajneesh were in control of the city, so they had access to the one and only decades-old fire truck. One of them ran to the firehouse and got the truck. They drove the truck to a water pipe used as a fire hydrant relatively close to the fire. So close that they stopped the vehicle over a burning bush. It would have been destroyed if the agent hadn't moved it. The fire truck and personnel were not very practical. Eventually, heavy equipment arrived. The local ranchers had bulldozers used in their work, and they often had to use it to fight fires, and they produced a good fire break. The fire burned itself out right at the edge of the playground for the school house.

There were lots of complaints from the locals about how the Rajneesh reacted to the fire. The most vehement complaint was about how the Rajneesh, who were vegetarians and, ironically in the light of the criminal charges, were not to kill anything were trying to shoo away or gather up the grasshoppers rather than getting down to business. There was no partnership created during or after the fire. The locals didn't trust the Rajneesh and the Rajneesh continued their aggressive techniques to harass them, trying to get them to move.

As I pondered the problem, it occurred to me that the Oregon Attorney General had instituted a lawsuit contending that the two cities, Antelope and the one on the ranch, were illegal because they were run by a religious organization. Perhaps we wouldn't need their approval after all.

The nail in the coffin was the AIDS scare. In the 1980's, the AIDS virus caused lots of fear in the world. There is no cure. There was nothing at that time that could hinder it once a person was infected. The Rajneesh were very concerned about it. On the ranch, they had spray bottles of disinfectant everywhere. They sprayed a phone and wiped it down before picking it up, and then spray and wipe down the receiver's ear and mouth pieces to ensure they were sterilized. Door knobs, window latches, anything that a person might touch, cough or even breathe on were sprayed and wiped.

When we visited, we were advised to use those precautions. I would watch as every time they picked up the phone or opened a door, even if they were the last person to use it, they would go through that cleansing ritual. I am told Rajneesh often spoke of the threat in his daily teachings to the followers.

How much of it was paranoia and how much was truth was debatable. One of the allowances of the Rajneesh was to have sexual encounters with multiple people. Given that was a major way the disease was spread, there was a danger of acquiring it. And how much was a genuine fear could be answered by Sheela's attacks on some of the followers that were trying to supplant her position within the Rajneesh.

During the criminal investigation, we found a series of housing units which were separated from the rest of the camp. These structures were occupied by Rajneesh followers who had been told they had the AIDS virus. These were enemies of Sheela, supporters of a faction trying to lessen her influence on Rajneesh.

They submitted to the isolation even though they couldn't be part of the ranch's communal activities because by being on the ranch they were close to the Bhagwan. They later found out that none of them had the virus. Actually, when you think about Sheela's abhorrent behavior, it was a wonder she hadn't infected them.

Taking advantage of the fear of the virus wasn't limited to Sheela's enemies at the ranch. She decided to create problems for the remaining non-Rajneesh residents of Antelope. Sheela and her gang had purchased some dormitory type cabins from another cult in Montana. They were brought in and placed on property within the City of Antelope.

Originally it was thought that they would be putting the street people who had been brought in to overload the vote in November 1984 in them. But they were not used for that purpose. Instead, they just dropped the homeless off in Madras, The Dalles, and Portland. However, Sheela and her minions concocted a more nefarious idea.

While the city itself had a small population, the property within the town limits was quite extensive. Knowing that, and that the county couldn't interfere with the property unless it were proven that the officials were corrupt, they decided they would have an AIDS colony in Antelope.

The summer of 1985 they came up with the idea that people with AIDS needed a place they could go since most citizens wanted them isolated to avoid being exposed to the virus. Sheela made a big deal about how they were going to set up medical facilities and invite anyone with AIDS to come to Antelope and live there. The Rajneesh would be providing free medical assistance to these patients in Antelope. It was a "humanitarian effort."

It was a credible threat, based on Sheela's past behavior. She was very spiteful. This kind of false compassion to help people, when in reality it was to intimidate and scare people, was a favorite weapon of hers. They never brought in anyone. I am not sure they ever intended to, or if it was just another thing to provoke the local citizenry and get them to move.

There were still a few people living in the town that were not Rajneesh, and I was getting reports from them that the Peace officers were still harassing them by putting spotlights in their windows late at night. They were following them anytime they left their residence, making them feel uncomfortable. If we could get enough evidence, we could charge them with official misconduct. I had a couple of citizens keeping track of the dates and times of the incidents. We were going to try and make a case, but the Rajneesh group disintegrated before we could do anything.

These were my reasons for not signing off on having their "24-hour dispatch" be a 9-1-1 center for Wasco County. In the end, it wasn't necessary to discuss it. There was a more pressing issue that came off and derailed their bid for the center.

All participants signed off on the plan. The Rajneesh were no longer involved. We moved forward purchasing the equipment with the remaining entities' 9-1-1 funds and setting it up in the phone company's building. Eventually, as a cost saving and more efficient use of manpower, the Center was placed under the Sheriff's Office.

The Board still met and discussed issues and directed the SO in modifications, but it was no longer a separate entity.

Soon after the fire, the time came when the influx of Rajneesh started coming into the ranch. As per my request, we received a daily report on the numbers coming in. I did find it interesting when we began receiving the population calls. We were told there were just a few hundred a day coming, when one day I noticed the Portland Oregonian quoted one of the leaders saying, "We have several thousand visitors coming in daily for the festival." I called the Chief and asked which was correct.

Seems that maybe they were over exaggerating to the media a bit or not giving us accurate information. Within the next couple of days, I saw numbers like three thousand, two thousand, etc. The numbers quickly totaled fifteen thousand, but it never went over it. Later after the festival, they would claim they had twenty thousand plus attend the festival. I questioned whether there were even 15,000 people in attendance. We had learned long ago that you could not rely on the honesty of the Rajneesh leaders. But I never saw them all in one place. Many reporters, however, had freer access to the property. They believed the numbers presented at the festival's peak attendance.

I was impressed with the planning of the festival. There was no expectation of violence or crime from the followers. But they were concerned, to a degree, of non-Rajneesh attending and creating problems. The Police would make any arrests, then they would turn the prisoners over to our Office. There were escape routes for the leaders of the commune, but they followed their normal evacuation plans.

The tents and additional buildings went up in just a few days. The followers had housing and transportation provided as part of the package. Members came from several different countries in Europe, Australia, China, Japan, and, of course, both American continents. Very few supporters arrived by private vehicle. Most came by air or train and public buses into the Portland area. The organizers would have Rajneesh school buses waiting at the Portland airport and other regions for the followers to catch and then ride out to the ranch.

They would be taken to the processing room, assigned quarters, and given their schedules. On the ranch, there were several bus stops within a few yards of where the visitors would be staying. Buses came by on a periodic basis and would pick up the followers to take them to the meetings, recreational areas and activities, and to their meals. For the most part, the festival was uneventful for us. The appointment of a Sergeant as a liaison with the Chief was a great assistance both for them and us.

By having the Sergeant go down each day and make himself available to the Police Department, it showed we were willing to work with them. He did a good job of meeting and talking with them. It also allowed him to get a feel each day as to how things were going. If there were any change in the tension between him and the Chief or other irregularities we hoped it would give us some warning of any future problems. The one flaw and it was serious, came about with the death of the Japanese National.

It was in the middle of the afternoon of July 3rd, a Wednesday when I received a phone call from the Reserve Deputy that had been at my first meeting.

She said, "We think we have had a drowning in the lake."

I asked, "You think you have?"

She said, "Yes, the report just came in that there was a man who has gone under the water and we can't find him."

I told her to have the Chief call me as soon as possible.

As required by state law, an accidental drowning must be investigated.

Our Sergeant was heading back up to The Dalles. He was on Bake Oven Road, a few miles from Shaniko and a good 45 minutes to an hour from the ranch. I told the dispatcher to have him go back to Shaniko and call me.

A few minutes later I had another call from the Reserve, she said there was definitely a drowning, and they had divers attempting to locate the man. He was Japanese and had come in from a city in Japan for the festival.

I asked her if they had any Deputy Medical Examiners at the ranch. I was pretty sure they didn't. This position was held by law enforcement officers who have gone through training AND had been appointed as such by the County Medical Examiner.

I had not heard that any had been appointed there. Again, there would be a question as to legality if they weren't an actual city. She didn't know. She did say the Chief was at the scene and would call me as soon as she could. That made sense. That was where I would have been.

I told the Reserve I would notify the County Medical Examiner and the District Attorney, I was pretty sure the CME would want the body brought up to The Dalles. She started arguing with me. I told her that it was state law.

Our District Attorney was easily found most of the time. This was one of the few times he had left the office early, and no one knew where he was. There was no Deputy DA. I didn't consider that a major problem, we were just required to notify him. We would continue to try and contact him.

I called Dr. John, the CME. I told him I had a Sergeant, who was a DME, and I would have him go to the scene. He said to have the body brought up to The Dalles for an autopsy. I then received a third call from the Reserve approximately 45 minutes after her first call.

She said, "The divers found the body and the ambulance crew worked on him and got him breathing again. They are taking him to the medical facilities."

A few minutes later I was called, by the Chief, and told that while the man was alive when they got him to the facility, he was worked on by the doctor who declared him dead. The doctor was a Jefferson County Assistant Medical Examiner. In the absence of the County

Medical Examiner, his authority was the same as one. He had to be approved by the State.

When I took that initial tour back in March, I wondered why every business and lodging facility was in Wasco County, and the medical facility was in Jefferson County. Now I knew.

She said that the young man had been swimming in the lake with some other Rajneesh. He had been gone from the shore to a large raft they had a few yards out. Suddenly he started thrashing water and then went down. It took them a while to find him, revive him and take him to the clinic where he died. I called Dr. John back up and told him where we were on the drowning, including the doctor on the scene being a Jefferson County Assistant Medical Examiner.

After a few cuss words and comments, which included my own thought of "you don't revive an adult who has been underwater that long in warm water in that heat," he said, "Bring the body up to The Dalles!"

The ranch had a large number of security personnel with semi-automatic weapons. I had a total of 12 deputies, of which only two were on duty. There was no way I was going to go down there and get the body, which was in Jefferson County, without further backup. That took time.

I told him that. I also said that the pronouncing physician was an Assistant Medical Examiner for Jefferson County. This trumped anything I could do, as the Sergeant was just a Deputy Medical Examiner. Dr. John thought for a moment and said he would contact the State Medical Examiner, who appointed the County Medical Examiners and his Assistants.

The State Medical Examiner was recently appointed as the Temporary State Medical Examiner. The former SMA had done some things that the Governor had felt were unethical and discharged him, appointing his Chief Deputy to replace him while they searched, nationally, for a permanent replacement.

His office couldn't find him. After about a half hour they finally located him, and he talked with Dr. John. He said he knew the Rajneesh doctor and trusted his judgment. Since the death "actually" occurred in Jefferson County it was his body and his case. If the Rajneesh doctor said it was an accidental drowning, that was good enough for him. Dr. John called me up, exasperated, saying leave him there.

The Sergeant reached Shaniko while I was making these calls and called me. By that time, it was evident to me that we would not be the investigating agency. I told him we lost because the "death," according to the doctor, took place in Jefferson County. It was ruled an accidental drowning closing the case.

I instructed him to go back down to the ranch, learn what he could and view the body to see if there was any sign of injury. He looked for any syringe marks, bruises, etc. that would indicate foul play. I would be in the office until I heard from him. I told Dr. John that the Sergeant would do the best he could to see if there was any problem, but, neither of us was hopeful.

The Sergeant got back to me a few hours later and said he couldn't see anything on the body that would arouse suspicion and those people he talked to said it had been an accident. No one had done anything to cause it. Our thoughts were not only physical foul play, but we wondered if someone had slipped something into his drink or food to cause him to not be able to take care of himself and drowned. Only a blood screen for alcohol and drugs would prove that, and to my knowledge, no blood was taken for analysis. We were all very frustrated.

I was scheduled to take my family down to Carla's folks' farm just out of Redmond for the Fourth of July weekend. We had a late start, but we headed down there. I had told the Sergeant that he didn't have to go down to the ranch on the fifth, I would be doing that. The fourth of July went fine. We sat under the stars and watch a fireworks display that was a few miles north of us.

Friday morning, the 5th, my Father-in-law and I headed out early to go to the ranch and make some rounds in South County. He had never been to the ranch so he was looking forward to the drive. We arrived at the ranch a little after 0900, and I met up with the Chief. She said this was the first body she had ever seen. She described him as young. He was about twenty-five if I recall right, but not a good swimmer. She said he looked "so peaceful" as he lay on the gurney in the clinic.

We talked for a while, everything on the ranch was going well according to her, and there were no obvious problems that I saw. We left the farm and headed north up to Antelope. It was quiet there so we passed on through, continuing north to Shaniko. In the middle of the switchbacks going up the hill, we met the OSP Lieutenant in charge of The Dalles office coming down.

He had another Lieutenant with him, and they were heading to the ranch. After a couple minutes talking we decided to go down to the little café/General store in Antelope (renamed Zorba the Buddha by the Rajneesh) and have some coffee. We got down there and found out it wouldn't be open for another hour or so. That was a huge relieve to my father-in-law. He wasn't looking forward to having anything from that little café.

The Lt. said that fireworks had caused a fire on a hillside in The Dalles, and it took a bit to put it out. While we were discussing it, two "Peace Officers" came up to talk. I told them that the Lt. was telling me about a fire caused by fireworks, and one of them started laughing and said we had our own 4th of July fireworks. Thinking that they probably shot off some over their lake, I mentioned that.

She said, "No, the boy that was drowned on Wednesday was cremated Thursday night, and sparks were just shooting out of the chimney." She thought it was great fun. I didn't.

CHAPTER 14

was still not comfortable about how that death was handled. But, even if I had thought it was funny I wouldn't have laughed. The Rajneesh were fond of making jokes and then taking offense if you laughed. The Lt. and I just looked at each other. I said I had to head out, and the Lt. stated that they did too, and we left.

We had lunch at the Oasis Café in Maupin. I had met the owner while campaigning. I liked him. His food was good and reasonably priced. He was an intelligent conversationalist. During the summer, he augmented their income as a Deschutes River guide and had clientele from as far away as New York City. The rest of the three hundred mile patrol went off without incident. We headed back to Redmond.

The first part of the following week we received a phone call from the US State Department. The Japanese Consulate had contacted them on behalf of the boy's parents, who were looking for him. The Rajneesh hadn't notified them of his death. Since it was Jefferson County's AME that declared the death, I told the State Department to call them. They could explain what had happened and why there was no investigation or autopsy. It was their headache, not mine.

Bill continually tried to work with the Rajneesh. A couple of weeks after the 1985 festival he and I went down to the ranch. They were supposed to have everything cleaned up and all temporary housing removed. It wasn't. There were still "temporary" buildings up and so on. He looked at me and said, "Now, don't holler at me, but I am giving them additional time."

He understood when I said, "Bill, that is one of the reasons they try and take advantage of you: you give too much leeway." The thing was he treated them like any other citizen. They needed extra time, no problem.

The problem, of course, was you give some people a leash, and they run with it. The Rajneesh were famous for doing just that. You couldn't let them take the bit between their teeth and run with it. It took an additional week before they had them down.

September 13, 1985 was the beginning of the end of Rancho Rajneesh. Unknown to most, Sheela left the country. On September 15th, in the afternoon, I was made aware that the Rajneesh was supposed to speak to his followers that evening. He had invited news media, State Police, our District Attorney and me to the meeting. I had one of the Sergeants attend too. I picked up the DA and headed to the ranch. We arrived about the same time an OSP Captain came, and we went into the meeting area together.

The news conference was held in the two-acre "greenhouse" turned meeting room. Several doors opened into the chamber from the south side. We were asked to sit in the front row on the south side of the platform where Rajneesh would be talking. The Rajneesh followers, still on the ranch, were dancing and singing to a small band as they waited for him to come.

There were several news reporters present. Rajneesh had been big news for some years, and this press conference was purported to be a significant development at the ranch. Rajneesh came into the room from a door leading to the back portion of the platform. He sat down in a large chair near the edge of the platform.

Smiling and looking around the room, he moved his arms up and down in time with the music then held up his hands for quiet. The band stopped, and he started speaking. This was the first time I had seen the man in person. He was not very tall. He had a long gray beard and hair, wearing a knitted cap of some kind. He was wearing expensive, long, flowing robes and a very expensive watch.

As he looked around the room his eyes were what I would call hypnotic, rarely blinking, and very piercing. He spoke good English but with slow, deliberate phrasing. While I cannot recall all that he talked about, the gist of it was that after Sheela had fled with her entourage a couple of days ago. On the 13th, her criminal conduct was uncovered. In front of him on tables were some items, mainly recording devices. He claimed that Sheela had caused these to be placed in the hotel, restaurant, and other areas where they could monitor and record conversations.

He was asked about the buildings in Antelope and he said it was all Sheela's idea, not his. He said something like, "I am the Guru of the rich, why would I want AIDS patients as part of my commune? They would cost us too much money," as he rotated the twenty-five thousand dollar watch on his arm.

He was asked about the restaurant poisonings in The Dalles. It was Sheela. The burning of the planning office. Sheela. Several other charges: the harassment, poisoning the commissioners, and others. He said that Sheela was the one who planned all of it. If you had asked him who killed JFK, he probably would have said Sheela. Most of the followers in the building were very surprised. They had no idea that these things had been done. And then having been done in the name of Rajneesh just added to their distress.

Those of us who had been dealing with the antics of Sheela and her group were not surprised. We had long suspected they were committing crimes but were unaware of the total extent. We did not trust them, and our feelings were now vindicated, particularly about the salmonella outbreak in The Dalles. This was germ warfare, and it has been declared the first mass attack of germ warfare on American citizens.

We looked at the "evidence" after he was done, but they weren't tagged and were useless as presented. Too many people had handled them, and the chain of custody had long been destroyed. However, as he accepted questions from the floor, he admitted that Sheela and her entourage had committed many crimes. The surface was barely scratched that night.

We had information, but it was all hearsay. We would have to formulate a plan to begin the investigation into Sheela's, and her henchmen's, activities. As we left the building to head home, the Chief came up to me. I looked at her, put my hands on her biceps and asked her one of the most satisfying questions I have ever asked, "What happened to your crime free city?"

"I don't know," she said. "I was wondering the same thing."

The next morning I arrived at the office and advised my detective sergeant as to what had happened the evening before. This would be a monumental investigation. It was a lot to take in. We were ready to formulate a plan.

As I was doing this, I received a phone call from the DA asking me to come to his office. We sat down with the FBI agent assigned to our area and talked over what had happened the night before.

It then occurred to us that we had not taken notes. However, the agent reached over to get the Oregonian Newspaper published that morning. He read off the charges. The paper had taken pretty good notes. It still left us with a void as to how we were going to begin. Together we decided to have the Chief of the force come up to The Dalles and see what she knew about the crimes.

I called down to talk to her and ask her to come up. Initially, I was met with resistance. The dispatcher said she was in the daily meeting with Bhagwan and would not be available for a couple of hours.

I asked her to have someone get her. The dispatcher said she wasn't available. I then asked her if she was refusing to contact the Chief and if she was ready to suffer the consequences for not doing so. A few minutes later the Chief called me. She would come up immediately. I asked her to meet us in the DA's office. When she arrived a few hours later, she brought with her the "city attorney" for Rajneeshpuram.

We then began to ask questions. She had been kept out of the loop of any of the allegations. While I can't recall what the City Attorney said, I remember that she wanted to be involved in the investigation, or at least informed as to what was going on. This was going to be massive. Wasco County did not have the resources to conduct it. We could not allow the Rajneesh "Peace Force" in on it either. We didn't know who was involved, and there was still a question as to the legality of the city and therefore the status of the Agency.

Later that afternoon, the Governor told us that he was invoking the statutes that allowed him to do investigations in lieu of local law enforcement. Neither the DA nor I was happy with his mandate.

I was the chief law enforcement officer of the county and to be told I could not lead the investigations was like a slap in the face. The DA felt the same about the usurping of his prosecution's role.

While I was not happy about relinquishing the primary investigative role to the Oregon State Police and the Attorney General's Office, we had no choice and didn't try to argue. My Office's resources were limited. I had just a few deputies, and the rest of the county had to be served. We still had activities going on, just like any other law enforcement office. We had accidents, crimes, calls to answer, papers to serve and the rest of the citizenry to protect.

The county did not have the financial resources to fund the investigation. It would require a great deal of overtime and bringing in other Sheriff's Deputies to augment my staff. I had some very good people. Not enough though. We didn't have the experience that would be required to undergo this investigation. It was going to be a massive undertaking.

This was to be an immense amount of work, requiring thousands of hours on-scene by a large contingency. While I didn't care about how this would be viewed nationwide, I knew that having the State involved would help keep the finger pointers at bay. The Rajneesh wouldn't be able to say the "local redneck biased County Sheriff" did the investigation, thus taking away the seriousness of the crimes.

At the time the investigation was the largest joint effort in Oregon's history, considering the task force, agencies and all the investigators involved. Dozens of people were involved, every day, in the investigation for several weeks and then for months afterward. We also brought in outside county and city agencies to augment our people on the ranch and perform some of the peripheral duties.

I do have to admit that the State Police and Attorney General's investigators did a good job. They included the deputies I assigned to the investigation at every step of the way. I was kept abreast on a day to day basis.

Back in 1985, we didn't hear about task forces. We had joint investigations, but that was different. Today, departments pair up on a regular basis to form Tasks Forces for complicated or major crime investigations.

The Rajneesh Crime Task Force consisted of four major groups. The FBI, which took on the wiretapping investigations. The INS continued their investigations on Immigration fraud. The State Police and Attorney General Investigators handled most of the other crimes. We came along for the ride, doing whatever we could to assist.

The lead agency was the Oregon State Police with a Lieutenant as the lead investigator. As a sheriff who would have been over his head as the investigation was conducted, I look back and wonder. The work would have been in addition to many other issues our office was facing at the time. It would have been too much to handle. My ego aside, the governor made a wise decision.

While there was always a possibility of violence against the investigators, none was threatened. Still, precautions were taken to ensure that they were as safe as possible. For the first few days, the investigators were being stonewalled by everyone. In order to get cooperation from the Rajneesh, we had to involve their Peace Force. Every morning we would meet in a meeting room, with the inclusion of the Chief and City Attorney. We would discuss the issues faced that day. At day's end, I would call the Attorney General, and we would discuss the investigation.

At night the investigators met in Madras to discuss the real issues and concerns and how they would proceed. This included a talk with the Attorney General. It was put out that if any of the Rajneesh had information they were to call a line that went to the Peace Force and they would relay it to the Task Force.

None of us thought that would work, but it would have the appearance of including the Peace Force and might make it more enticing for the people to call. That process was tested by investigators and found that a lot of the information did not get very far. As Rajneesh people were talked to, they stated that they had left messages with and given information to the Peace Force. The task force had not received them.

We were concerned about the destruction of evidence, but we didn't have enough information. For several days issues remained unaddressed as to where the information was on the ranch. Thanks to a couple of AG investigators taking the tour offered to anyone interested, we got the last bit of information necessary to obtain warrants.

The night before we were to serve them we met in Madras to formulate a plan. The next day the Task Force received better cooperation from the Rajneesh, so the Lt. chose not to serve the warrants at that time. Tuesday they went back to the stonewalling. It was decided that we would serve the warrants on Wednesday.

I contacted several Sheriff's Offices and the City of The Dalles PD. since the City had been under attack, it was only fair that they participate. In addition there were extra officers from the State Police and AG's Office, as well as FBI agents. That morning there was over eighty law enforcement personnel on the ranch, not counting twelve to eighteen of us in the morning meeting room, ready to serve the warrants.

We met that morning in the meeting room as usual around a large oval table. At the head of the table was the State Police Superintendent. I sat down at the far end of the table across from him. I was an observer of the drama that was about to unfold.

In the morning meeting, a private attorney for one of the Rajneesh had asked to address the group and was given permission to be there. He said his client had a lot of information to give if she would be granted immunity. According to him, she could bust the case wide open.

He didn't like the Chief investigator for the AG and belittled him whenever he could. He tried to get the investigator to listen to him about his client. The investigator wouldn't. He had plenty of other information and didn't need hers. The attorney insisted on talking with one of the two AG attorneys that were assigned to the case. They refused to meet with him.

What he didn't know was the two men were in a motor home along with a SWAT team just east and alongside the building. We were not about to tell him. In addition to that vehicle and the vehicle transporting those deputies, officers, and agents to the scene, we had other vehicles that would help ensure the best communication possible as well as protection for the investigators.

For communications, we had the one tower OSP had for radio transmission in the valley area of the farm. But we also had a couple of communications rigs, one in the valley and the other about half way up the road going into the ranch proper. The second one would be used as a relay site for the first one to other transmitters. Both of these units were OSP's. Plus, the relay also had a SWAT team in it.

The National Guard was put on standby by the Governor just in case. Somehow a reporter had found out about the Guard and had published the information. He said his source was me. It was not, I had not talked to the man. I called his editor and complained, for whatever good it did.

His information was accurate on some issues, and he put the security of the officers at risk. I had moved our communications truck, such as it was, onto another ranch a few miles out from the property just in case. The ranch belonged to a former commissioner, current budget committee member, and a good friend.

After several minutes of demanding his client be given immunity, the attorney, in exasperation, proclaimed in a smug voice and attitude, "Okay then, all these officers you have standing around here today? They are not going to have anything to do!"

The Superintendent then turned to the Lt., sitting to his left and said, "Show him."

The Lt. pulled the warrants out and gave the locations we would be searching, laying them down one at a time. The attorney looked around the table and then back at the Superintendent. "I guess that is that then," the attorney said.

CHAPTER 15

Both the Chief and the City Attorney were surprised and upset. The CA told the Chief that she was not to participate in the searches. She was to have officers watch the investigators as they executed the search warrants. This was the end of those morning meetings. Of course, they had been a sham and not really needed.

Each day, about 1600 hours, the Lieutenant would hold a news conference on the status of the investigation. I was there one day. Afterward, a young man came up and asked if I would be willing to live in the commune. I am not sure just what he was trying to get out of me. I told him no, it was too far away from the office, where I had to be each day. He kept asking questions, I kept pointing out the same problem.

I kept my eye on him as he blended back into the crowd. I could see him talking to the editor of the Rajneesh Times, shaking his head as he did so. She looked up and saw me watching them and turned away. I liked her, by the way. While she maintained the party line, she also seemed to try and listen to what we said and asked good questions.

It was interesting to me that instead of asking for herself she sent someone else. She had never been bashful about that in the past. My comments were valid, but I had learned a long time ago that we could not always trust what we were asked or what we heard from the Rajneesh. I chose not to elaborate. I had no idea how my remarks were going to be interpreted. If this had been an attempt at a trap, I heard no more from them.

Tons of evidence was seized. There were dozens of boxes used to carry the evidence off the ranch to The Dalles. Evidence included the same salmonella strain that was used in the attack to poison citizens of The Dalles back in 1984. Bugs were found in phones, of both the Ranch's private lines and the pay phones for people to call out on. Bugs were inserted in the hotel rooms so well that it took the FBI a long time before they could find them. Both the equipment and tapes were seized. Charges were filed in Federal Courts.

A house across the street from the County Courthouse was vacant. The investigation rented it. The site became the processing point for all the information. It also contained the offices for the two AG Attorneys for over a year.

Interviews were conducted. As the rank and file realized the extent of Sheela's betrayal to the commune, more Rajneesh came forward. The enormity of the crimes committed in the name of the Rajneesh shocked them. They wanted the perpetrators punished as much as the county citizens.

The vast majority of the Rajneesh had come to the commune in search of an answer to their spiritual needs. They contributed their savings and their labor so that the ranch would be successful. They envisioned the rest of their life being spent with other Rajneesh. These leaders had destroyed that dream. These people that they had trusted tarnished not only their name but that of the commune. In the growing light of this betrayal, followers cooperated in droves with the investigation any way they could.

The investigators wanted to interview Rajneesh himself. His attorneys tried to look like they were cooperating, but they weren't getting him in the forefront. Rajneesh had allergies. The lawyers started laying down the rules the investigators must follow to see him, among them taking showers to make sure all cologne was gone, and wearing the robes of the followers so their clothes wouldn't affect him. Rajneesh's attorney wanted the investigators to treat him as a deity.

The investigators said it wasn't worth it and refused to comply with their requests. If the investigators needed his testimony, they could subpoena him. They weren't concerned about the obstructive actions. They had enough from his original statements and the statements of Rajneesh followers to obtain warrants. And they had another ace in the hole yet to be played.

A lot of things were going on behind the scenes, much of which I wasn't privileged to, but it did cause some turmoil for the lead investigators of the Federal and State agencies. One of the frustrations I encountered as the local law enforcement was that State and Federal authorities often worked on the same things we worked on without sharing their information or plans. There were reasons, of course, but it can be exasperating nonetheless. As time went on, I found out that there were things that had been going on for some time to monitor the Rajneesh's activity by state officials. This monitoring was not shared with us.

The Attorney General was the most forthcoming State Official, but even he had withheld information.

As often happens, one Federal agency didn't know what another Federal Agency was doing, leaving the state out of the loop as well. All of us like to protect our turf and information, but it was incredible when you have something as significant as this investigation, that they wouldn't share with each other. While it would have been nice to have known, and we could have shared more and shed light on shadows the state wasn't aware of long before the investigation began, in the end, it didn't matter.

On October 28th, 1985, Bhagwan and some of his closest confidants fled the ranch, leaving the rest of the followers behind.

Now, the following narrative has some basis in facts which are verifiable. However, much of it is speculation on my part, some based on unconfirmed information and some from watching the systems play out.

Fact: INS had been investigating the Rajneesh and his followers for several years because of immigration fraud.

Fact: He was bringing in people from other countries, India being the main one, and marrying them off to Americans so they could remain in the states. The marriages were shams.

The rest is speculation and hearsay, based on information I heard during and soon after the investigation. I don't recall from whom I obtained it thirty years ago. That said, this information represents everything I remember from that time.

There were claims that there was a mole in the INS offices, that information of their investigations was being leaked to the Rajneesh and that it had been going on for several years. There was speculation that, just before his announcement of Sheela's betrayal, Rajneesh was being warned that an arrest warrant was coming soon.

To try and endear himself to Federal officials and get those charges dropped for his cooperation, he may have sent Sheela out of the country so she would be out of harm's way when he made his announcement in September.

People agreed to come forward and give information. As enough information came to the State and Federal prosecutors, Wasco County and Federal grand juries were convened. Secret indictments were issued.

Warrants were obtained. Some of those indicted had already fled the country. Investigators needed to coordinate all arrests so those didn't get tipped off and go to a country that did not have extradition treaties.

However, as the Bhagwan Rajneesh and his advisers watched the investigation they knew he was in trouble. Search warrants had been executed with tons of evidence gathered. Most of his followers were now being cooperative. The investigators became less interested in what he had to say, and by inference unwilling to grant him immunity for the INS crimes.

"Somehow" he learned of a warrant charging him with the Immigration violations that had been issued. Knowing he would soon be served, in a matter of days at most, he was on a jet flying out of state.

I "think" the leak of his impending arrest was given to the mole to get the information to Rajneesh. Here is why:

It was late in the fall. The population at the ranch was dwindling. Still, they had a large security force at the ranch. These men and women were well armed, as was the Peace Force. Rajneesh's followers believed, and many still do, that he had no part in these crimes. The facts remain. Sheela relayed everything she did to him on a daily basis. Her power remained only while she had his ear. His death proves he wasn't a god. The facts of the case suggested he was aware of what was going on. Still, for the purposes of the investigation, it was their mindset that was important.

These followers had no idea of what was going on in the background, but they were loyal to Rajneesh. Arresting him and taking him to jail while he was on the ranch would have been asking for trouble, maybe even gunfire. There was no point in risking anyone's life over these charges. It would be better for everyone if they could get him off the property. Thus, the leak.

His advisors obtained the information and ran with it, literally. They contacted a private corporation to get a jet onto the ranch fast. If my memory serves me, it was based in one of the smaller communities near Portland, but I am not sure of that.

The jet flew into the ranch. The Rajneesh and entourage got on it and were flown out of Oregon. They weren't thinking. They were in panic mode and forgot that pilots have to file a flight plan. This pilot, flying for a reputable company, did so.

They landed in Charlotte, North Carolina. He was far away from his security force with little risk of injury to anyone. Rajneesh was arrested without incident. Now for a bit of information that I received from the pilot a few years later. I met him while I was a member of an informational committee sent around the state to meet with US Congressmen to tell them what the North Deschutes River Management agreement contained.

A lot of work had been done. A committee made up of over 20 agencies and private citizens, representing groups such as river guides, fishing organizations, etc. met several times over several years discussing the issues, gathering information, and coming to a consensus of how the river should be managed. I was the representative from Wasco County on the Committee. I was asked to participate in the meetings with Congressmen and/or their staff. The committee gave the presentation from the State, from the Bureau of Land Management, and a couple other reports that I cannot recall.

We wanted to get the information out in one day, so we rode in a BLM contracted jet. The pilot that flew us that day was the one that flew Rajneesh off of the ranch in 1985. He told me his firm received the call, and he was assigned. He arrived early that day.

The followers removed some seats and installed the Rajneesh's personal chair, a throne like he used while seated to lecture his supporters in the "greenhouse."

He said that the Rajneesh was high on something. It was known that he partook of Nitrous oxide, laughing gas, on a regular basis in the privacy of the compound. The pilot didn't know what he was on, but he didn't think that was it because it lasted for several hours.

They flew out of the ranch and headed South East. The followers started asking him to fly to Bermuda (or the Bahamas, I can't recall which). They wanted Rajneesh out of the country. He told them that he couldn't. First, he didn't have enough fuel. Second, an over water flight required two pilots, and he was the only one on board. Third, equipment mandated for flights over large bodies of water, for use in the case of a water crash, was not part of the equipment on the jet. It would have to be secured before they could fly out of the country.

Regardless, he would have to land in North Carolina to fuel because he had insufficient fuel to fly that far. The jet was tracked. I heard there were a couple of Air Force jets that accompanied him without the pilot's knowledge. And, I heard the FAA tracked them as they flew cross country. Either way, the agencies knew where he was at all times.

Upon landing at Charlotte, the pilot found himself staring down a rifle barrel aimed by a deputy. The local authorities knew of the weapons the Rajneesh had access to and were not taking any chances. The authorities kept telling him to get his hands up. He kept telling them he had to shut down the plane. They let him. The authorities took Rajneesh into custody and placed him in a cell.

At the time, the pilot said he wore his hair long and had a beard, typical of the area. The company jacket he had on was red, one of the Rajneesh colors. The pilot went into the cell right along with Rajneesh. They thought he was part of the commune.

He stated that Rajneesh was out of it, making unintelligible statements. He remained that way for several hours, and he still was not lucid when the pilot was released hours later, after the pilot's story checked out. He was released and flew back home.

The flight from the ranch occurred on October 27, 1985. Rajneesh did not arrive back in Oregon until November 7 or 8th, 1985, eleven or twelve days later.

I am speculating, not because I know anything, but because it makes sense. At least to me. The reason for the long delay was authorities wanted to ensure the Bhagwan Rajneesh understood what incarceration would be like.

At the ranch, Bhagwan Rajneesh was treated like a god. He was the center of attention, and everyone worshiped him. The Bhagwan could do no wrong. His every desire was met. He had Rolls Royces to drive, expensive clothes and jewelry to wear. Anything he wanted was given to him. Not only was he living a life of luxury, but the whole commune centered on him. The community existed for his pleasure. Now, he was in the custody of the Federal Government. His life took a one hundred eighty degree turn.

There were three ways of transporting prisoners. They can travel in smaller vehicles like cars or vans, by bus, or by plane. If they use the vans or buses, most prisoner transporting goes from point A to point B with several stops along the way, so that point B becomes point Z. They drive during the day, stopping at a jail or prison where the prisoners stay locked up overnight.

When they stop at these facilities, they release some prisoners to local agencies and take others onto the vehicle to transport them down the line to the location, and the authorities, where they committed their crimes. It was a less expensive way to move prisoners than flying since each agency doesn't have to take the time, manpower or expenses to go long distances to get their own prisoners.

It wasn't done for all prisoners. Sometimes it was critical that a person was transported fast, and/or the agency that was investigating the crime wants their officers to take custody of the prisoner at the place of arrest, for interrogation purposes. But, for the rest, the prisoner transport system works just fine even though it takes time. It wasn't just a leisure jaunt across the continent.

The prisoner would be cuffed and often wear leg irons to make it more difficult for them to escape. They would not stop at rest stops, and they do not take the scenic route. The prisoners had no say in who their companions would be in the vehicle. There may be a non-violent felon sitting next to a murderer. The only thing they might have in common would be the process.

The trip would make several stops each day along the way. Instead of a few hours, or a couple of days to go cross-country, it could take several days, even a week or more. It was my understanding that Rajneesh was transported on such a bus, if so that would explain the time between the arrest and the arrival in Portland.

Now, if the transport were up to me, I would have wanted to give him a good taste of prison life, but make sure he wouldn't be injured. They didn't need a martyr for the followers. Safety for any prisoner was a concern. I would surround him with agents acting as prisoners. He would be treated like a detainee, not a god. He would have to deal with criminal elements, stay in a cramped cell, and eat bland food.

Nothing life-threatening, of course. He would have to take his showers and other personal hygiene activity in the company of several men.

He would have no privacy. His every movement would be monitored, and he could not control his activities. He would even have to ask permission to visit the toilet, with no privacy. He would have no control over anything. He would be without the support and adoration of his followers. He would be just one prisoner among many; one face in a crowd.

The time would be an education like he had never experienced and was not prepared to endure. They could give him a good feel for what it would be like, but he would be in no danger. I'm not saying that was what they did, but it is what I would have done. In my mind, it was a real possibility given that within a few days of his arrival in Portland he pled guilty to Immigration violations.

The end result was he was fined and allowed to leave the country. The investigation and interviews of other members continued for several weeks. People made deals and gave up information that was helpful to the agencies. Other people not involved in any of the crimes came forward with their statements as to what they had observed over the years.

No automatic weapons had been found, but there was a report from one of the followers that the Rajneesh had obtained some illegally. They had been dumped in a pond on the property. The pond was small but deep enough to require scuba gear. One of our deputies was a diver and he, along with another deputy from Jefferson County, as I remember, were assigned to the search.

The water was stagnant, full of green scum. The two men searched for a couple of hours but were never able to find anything. Both deputies became very sick from the contaminated water and had to be off work for a few days. The danger wasn't only to come from a loaded gun in the hands of an angry security officer.

CHAPTER 16

Over twenty Rajneesh were indicted with varying State and/or Federal crimes. The charges ranged from the Federal accusations of electronic eavesdropping and immigration violations to the State allegations of poisoning, arson, violations of election laws, conspiracy to commit murder, and attempted murder, to name a few.

Except for two followers, the suspects were charged with both Federal and State crimes. The Federal government took "possession" and paid the related costs for those suspects.

However, the two that had only State charges became the responsibility of the Wasco County Sheriff's Office. That became a problem for us. We did not have space for them. We had to farm them out. The adjoining county of Hood River could hold only one of them. Multnomah County was able to hold the other one. They could have held both, but their daily costs of housing a prisoner was twice Hood River's. I housed one in each facility.

To accommodate the attorneys, we would "rotate" the prisoners. They would usually appear in Multnomah County for court at the same time. At the request of one attorney the prisoner that was in Hood River County would then be switched for the prisoner in Multnomah County, facilitating meetings with their respective attorneys to make it less time-consuming and less costly to the County. Within a few months, both prisoners pled guilty and were sentenced by the court. The State Corrections Division then took charge of them.

The incarceration of the two cost Wasco County over $25,000. It had to be removed from the Contingency funds of the County Budget. It was part of funds set aside for overruns the county departments might have, but it dug into the reserves of the county. The Rajneesh were still causing us financial losses. However, there was an unexpected "windfall" a year or two later.

The Rajneesh had a hotel in Portland. It would house followers going to and coming back from the ranch while they waited for transportation. It also housed those followers who had business to take care of in Portland. This was the visible property they had, they also had houses in Portland where they could go unobserved and used them to help conceal their identities and plan nefarious deeds against some of the Federal and other officials.

I don't remember when or why, but the State of Oregon seized the hotel. They then put it up for sale. Multnomah County purchased the property. They used it as a halfway house in dealing with inmates.

The AG's Office contacted me and asked how much the county had to pay for the lodgings of the two followers while they were in WCSO custody. I gave them the costs. The State then reimbursed Wasco County for those expenses. They didn't have to do that, but it was very much appreciated by everyone. The one added irony, one which I always chuckle over, was that Multnomah County paid our costs of housing the prisoners in Multnomah County's jail, back to us with the purchase of the hotel.

The results of the investigation would be felt, and more interviews would be conducted, for several years. As would the impact on the county and the Sheriff's Office.

Many of the followers left the area and moved on to other communities. Some remained loyal to the Rajneesh commune. Even today, 30 years later, they still read and share his works. Some stayed in the area. They moved to The Dalles and other communities around us. They have integrated into the communities, and most of us have no idea of their background with Rajneesh. It isn't important to know. They are productive citizens and contribute to the general welfare of the communities. Some still follow his teachings, others have moved on.

They should be able to live in peace. These people had no idea of what their leaders did until later. They were not part of Sheela's grand scheme. But I'm getting ahead of myself. During the investigations of the ranch, K.D. became a star witness against the other leaders and turned state evidence. He went into the witness protection program.

K.D. was an arrogant person. He was a key figure in the operation of, the guidance of, and planning of the violence against the citizens. He was the Mayor of the ranch when I met with the Chief in 1985. He had a demeanor about him that showed he thought he was superior to everyone else. More than once, Bill was the recipient of K.D.'s sneers and sarcasm.

One day, a few years after the investigation, he was brought back to the courthouse to give a deposition. He was in our basement meeting room with the Marshals who had brought him and the state attorneys.

Bill asked me to go with him to see K.D. I did so. Nothing was said between the two men. Bill knew of the criminal assault against him and on several other people. He was aware that they put the citizens of Wasco County and many in other parts of Oregon at risk. Bill knew K.D. was a significant portion of that illegal operation.

As we went back upstairs, Bill said, "Art, I just cannot stand that man. I have prayed about it for years, but I still cannot stand him." This bothered him on a level that I still cannot understand. To me, it speaks so many volumes about the man. He didn't like feeling that way about another person. That was Bill. That was why I respected his leadership and the life he lived.

As far as our Office was concerned our work regarding the Rajneesh was complete. Then I received a phone call at home from a long-time resident of Antelope. The Rajneesh had tried to get some of the townspeople to accept a seat on the City Council. No one would agree to an appointment.

The Rajneesh had shut down the ranch to leave. It was pretty much abandoned in early December. They said they wanted to give the community back to the residents. To that end, they put back the removed road signs from a few years earlier.

When they took over the town, they had named all the streets for different people like Buddha and other names that the Rajneesh valued. This was their way of showing contempt for the local citizens at that time. Now the streets were back to their old names. It was the Rajneesh's white flag.

The caller had asked me to come down and take possession of all the paperwork and the firearms that were in City Hall. They wanted them taken for safe keeping. The locals didn't trust the Rajneesh. They didn't know if they had done some things that could come back on the City and them personally if they accepted an appointment from the Rajneesh city council. The locals didn't want to be caught in the middle of a last ditch attempt at retaliation by the Rajneesh. They were afraid any fines or penalties might attach to them.

There was a process in Oregon if a City loses all its city council. The citizens request the County Commission appoint a mayor, who will then appoint a councilman. The two would appoint a third, and so it would go until all positions were filled.

Antelope had a five-person council. It was a lot for such a small population of at max forty people, but that was what the charter required. The Mayor announced to the media that the then-council members would all resign their positions on the same day I was asked to retrieve the arms. The meeting was scheduled for that morning at either 0900 or 1000.

They held their meetings in the basement of the Antelope school house. The meeting room was packed out by local citizens; not just the city people, but many of the local ranchers also came.

In the ranching world of South Wasco County, these ranchers were all neighbors, knew each other, helped each other out in times of trouble and supported each other as they ran their ranches. Their nearest neighbor could be 15 miles up the road, but they were all neighbors if they lived down there.

These ranchers included a big burly man named John Conroy. John was in his 60's and was as thick as he was wide. He stood about 5'10. In the old days of football, he would have been a great fullback. He was an Eastern Oregon Rancher, solid as they came. He didn't talk much and didn't mince words when he did. John's cattle ranch was off Bake Oven Road, a county road that ran between Maupin to just south of Shaniko. His ranch was about 30 – 35 miles from Antelope.

John had been a County Commissioner. He was also a Budget Committee member for the county. That was where I first met him.

Like most cattlemen in that part of the county his ranch was large; several thousand acres, as I recall. He also rented BLM land adjacent to his for additional cattle grazing. The land was rugged and much like the Big Muddy: lots of sagebrush, juniper and bunch grass which fed the cattle in the field.

He had hay fields and pastures mixed in, but the bulk of the property would be considered barren. Lush greenery requires water as well as a soil to produce it. This area of the county didn't have much water. It was desert sand. One only improved patches as needed.

He was a character. During one of the Budget Meetings, I was coming in to present our Budget to the committee. Just ahead of me was the County trapper who was in charge of predator control.

His job was to trap and kill coyotes before they attacked the livestock. Most of his work took place in South County since that was where the problem needed to be addressed. He didn't have a large budget, and it was just there to supplement the work.

Coyotes can kill young calves and lambs. Livestock ranchers will tell you that they will grab hold of one and rip it open and then go to the next one, without eating the first. But it isn't just the livestock that was in danger.

The Committee chairman was a cherry grower whose orchards

were close to The Dalles. As the presentation of the trapper was concluded, the chairman said he didn't understand why we needed to have coyotes killed.

He then went on about how those coyotes around his orchards were considered pets. They were friendly critters who had a beautiful voice as they sang to the moon. He was making a big deal about how nice they were. You could see John getting red in the face. He was about ready to explode.

The chairman was pulling his leg. He looked over at John and said, "But then I didn't have my wife's pet dog grabbed off the back porch by a coyote, either." They approved the trapper's budget.

Then it came time for me to present the Sheriff's Budget. As I talked, the noon fire alarm went off. John looked at his watch and said, 'Oh, it's 1100."

I said, "No, it is 1200, John, that was the noon whistle."

Like most ranchers, he didn't much care for Daylight Savings Time and left his watch on standard time. The cattle didn't recognize the hour change, so he didn't either.

He looked at me and smiled, "So your noon whistle goes off at 1100, huh?" He got me hook, line and sinker. I got back at him later, though.

John didn't much care for the "modern day conveniences" of city life. I was told he would give the city folk a bad time about all the things they had to endure, the hated parking meters being one of them. He said he did just fine without those, and the other contraptions city folk had to deal with.

For his birthday his friends had rounded up an old phone booth, a parking meter, and a fireplug and put it on the entrance to his driveway just off Bake Oven Road. He left them up.

On one of my trips to the Ranch, I noted that he had left a car parked next to the fire hydrant. I gave him a parking ticket for the offense and another for parking at an expired meter. I phonied them up, of course, so they weren't valid.

He enjoyed the prank, he said, but he wasn't too happy, at first, finding two tickets on his car. That was a snapshot of John, a no-nonsense rancher. He was at that meeting in Antelope that morning. When the Mayor had concluded his remarks and asked again for some of the City's citizens to take over, without success. He then said the meeting was adjourned.

There were a number of reporters there that morning and several questions were asked. The best question came from John. He asked the Mayor, "Are you going to apologize to the citizens?"

Taken aback by the question, the Mayor said, "No, I haven't done anything to apologize to the citizens for."

He had taken over the post right before the final days. He was about the 4th or 5th Mayor since K.D. was arrested. John replied that he believed the Rajneesh as a group owed the citizens an apology. The Mayor made it clear he wasn't going to apologize.

One of the reporters from a Portland television station had a cameraman with her. She had set up to cover the council and heard John's question. They hadn't recorded John since the mike wasn't on him and the camera was pointed away.

As everyone was leaving, she approached John. She asked him to repeat the question. He said no.

She was a pretty young lady. She tried using all her feminine wiles to coax him into it. She said that they didn't know he was going to ask, so they hadn't been able to record him.

He said, "No, I know how you people work. You ask a question, and then you keep asking. I won't ask it again."

The young reporter was persistent. "All I want is the question on camera. I promise you I won't ask anything else."

It took several long minutes of pleading, but in the end, she got him to agree.

I just stood back enjoying her maneuvering and working on this crusty old rancher.

She said, "Okay, what I am going to do is ask you what you said, and you ask your question." She almost had him. Almost. However, she said, "And then…"

John cut her off and said, "See, I told you, you would do that. I am not going to ask the question."

She pleaded a bit longer, but she realized too late that she had blown it. I just stood back and smiled. We had seen a lot of her through the summer as her station recorded incidents about the Rajneesh. She looked over at me, by now grinning from ear to ear and just gave that "well, I tried" smile, shook her head and left.

Afterward, I joined the retired Mayor at City hall to take possession of the keys, paperwork, and weapons the Rajneesh had purchased with Antelope city funds. Can't remember how many side arms, nor what they were. I just remember the AR-15.

I thought to myself, why in the world would this little town need such firepower? Since they had plenty on the ranch. The one thing I did note was that they had returned everything, and from what I heard they had not taken anything they shouldn't have. Proof that not all of them worked outside the law.

I placed the boxes of files in the County Road Department's garage there in the city. I called the County Judge and Road Master and asked permission right after I received the call. I placed the firearms in the trunk to take back and secure at our office. This was as the citizens had requested. Later they requested that I sell the guns at public auction. All the funds went back to the city.

I headed on down to the ranch and passed a few cars coming out. One young man walked up the hill as I went down. The "city" was now a ghost town. There were caretakers still on the property, and they stayed there until the ranch was foreclosed on. There were not many of them, and all they could do was maintain part of the facilities. They chose to work at Rajneesh's private area.

As I headed back up, I stopped and picked up the young man who was walking. He headed to Madras and then south. I gave him a ride to Antelope and then he went south towards Madras from there. He told me that he had been at the ranch almost from the beginning. He had worked long and hard, 12 hour days, 7 days a week as most of them did, to help the commune build the facilities, plant crops and whatever needed to be done.

I said, "Must be frustrating. You wasted four years of your life on the ranch; now it is nothing."

He said what I had heard from some of the other members. "No, it wasn't a waste. I got to be near the Master and listen to him every day."

If this had been me, and I'd been able to spend four years with my "god," walking and talking each day, I wondered if I would feel the same way.

CHAPTER 17

We talked some more as we drove to Antelope. He told me that he didn't always understand what Rajneesh was saying. "One day he would say one thing and the next something else that contradicted what he had said the previous day. But, what he said was the truth at the time he said it."

I just shook my head. Later that month I attended a Sheriffs' conference. I related how the people of Antelope had appreciated my coming down and helping them.

One wise older sheriff said, "Art, it only takes one 'oh no' to wipe out a hundred of those 'good job, Sheriff' remarks."

He spoke from experience, and, now, so can I. He was right.

Sheela was captured in Germany and brought back to the United States to stand trial. She first was tried in the Federal Courts and sentenced, and she pled guilty to the state charges.

She was to serve her time in a Federal facility, after which she would serve her state crimes in a state facility.

A few months before she was released I received a call from the Attorney General's Office. They wanted to bring Sheela up to our county to interrogate her on what she had done with some of the money she had taken, among other things.

The state was going to pay the costs of transportation, but they would like me to go with them. Also, since it was my county and my Corrections Manager was a female, I was asked to bring her with me.

On a Friday that week we flew into San Francisco, rented a car, and drove the twenty or so miles to Pleasanton Penitentiary, a Federal facility.

The Penitentiary was named for the town, but it fit the minimum security feel of it. The facility would be one that people call a "Country Club."

Rules were looser, and there was plenty of activity for the inmates to enjoy.

We arrived at about 1600 hours and went to the warden's office. He said he hadn't been informed by Washington that we were coming and couldn't release her to our custody without their permission. And of course, everything was closed back there since it was three hours later.

The Attorney General's office had contacted the Federal Prison Bureau and let them know we would be down to pick up Sheela. Everything had been approved; not sure why the warden didn't receive the message.

Rather than flying back and then having to repeat the trip we rented motel rooms. We then toured San Francisco on Saturday and my brother-in-law, a Police Officer for the City of Alameda across the bay from San Francisco, drove us around the countryside, showing different areas not normally seen by the average citizen.

One of the areas I wanted the Corrections Manager to see was the Redwoods. She came from South Dakota and had never seen such monsters.

Monday we picked Sheela up and transported her back to The Dalles. She "enjoyed" the trip. She had "forgotten how pretty the Gorge was," etc.

We booked her into our facility so she was on record of being held by Wasco County, and then transported her to Hood River Jail to wait until the attorneys wanted to talk to her.

We brought her back to The Dalles where they interrogated her in our meeting room. While they didn't get much from her, they did disrupt her schedule. That made her unhappy, as she missed her tennis match.

We took her back and came back home.

A few months later she was to be released. The Pleasanton Warden was to contact the State Corrections Department the day before Sheela was released from Federal Custody so they could have a Transport team pick her up and take her to a State Prison the day of her release.

They didn't call until the day AFTER she was released, claiming that there had been a clerical error, and they were "sorry."

Needless to say, the Corrections Department and Attorney General's Office personnel were very upset. They filed a complaint with the overseer of the federal prison system, but not much came to it as far as Oregon was concerned.

She had hopped a plane for Switzerland (or Sweden, I don't recall which for sure), a non-extradition country, the same day she was released and was safely tucked away where the State could not get her.

It is my understanding that she is still there today, to avoid arrest. She runs a Nursing Home.

You've got to wonder.

In 1989 the ranch went into foreclosure. During the preceding years, it had gone into bankruptcy and receivership. A lot of the items left behind were sold to pay off debts.

When Sheela left, and it became apparent that the ranch was going to go down, our County Treasurer had us post notices on the portable items that were taxed by the county, such as the trailers. If/when sold, taxes must be paid before anyone could take possession.

I remember meeting with one of the bankruptcy trustees on one of my trips down to the ranch. He said he was impressed with the quality of the workmanship. Everything was built to code, even if they had built it all illegally. The Rajneesh had used a lot of local businesses, including from The Dalles and Madras, to purchase items. It was a way they had tried to endear themselves to people.

In the beginning, they paid cash for delivery. One business that profited from this arrangement was a Propane dealer in Madras. He was a friend of my dad. One day, he and I had a conversation about his contacts and business dealings with the Rajneesh. He had several propane tanks on the property. He rented them to the Ranch and was paid every time gas was delivered, including the rental on the tanks.

He was in his office one day when some Rajneesh came in wanting him to help them with heating the "greenhouse" turned meeting hall. There were formulas for determining what would be needed to heat a building. They also help with the best location of those heaters. When he asked them the size, they said two acres.

He said he thought about that for a couple seconds then said, "I don't know, I have never been asked to figure heat by the acre before."

Of course, that broke down to almost 90,000 square feet, and he was more than happy to help them with their heating of the "greenhouse;" it brought in more money for him. And since it was cash on delivery, he was never at risk of losing any money.

When the Rajneesh declared they were closing the ranch, he had his crew go down and get all the tanks back to Madras. It took a bit of time and more than one trip, but he got them all back.

While the propane dealer did not suffer any losses, others were not so fortunate. Once the Rajneesh established their willingness to pay, they had some of the items and work done on credit. However, later, they stopped paying the vendors altogether. Several businesses lost a lot of money because of the Rajneesh's bankruptcy. Some went out of business because they couldn't sustain the loss.

By fall of 1988, all the legal work for the foreclosure was complete. The ranch was to be sold on the steps of the Wasco County Courthouse.

The week before the sale some of the Rajneesh invited the public and the news media to come down to the ranch for one last meeting. Those that were still there and a few that would come from outside the ranch were still trying to save what they'd built. But they knew it was gone, and they wanted one last press conference to say farewell to their property.

Bill told me about the meeting. He talked me into going. We left that morning. While we were there waiting for the Rajneesh to open the area up, I received information that there was someone close to the area with a gun. They had already called the Sheriff's Office.

One of our deputies was close by and made contact with the person, I stayed outside for a few minutes. We had radio contact with each other to make sure he was okay. He was. The man was a hunter on BLM property. The rest of the people and Bill had gone into the meeting area. I came into the room and saw Bill sitting back in a corner and joined him. He admonished me, "Don't ever leave me alone with these people."

After all, he had gone through I couldn't blame him. I had told him what I was going to do when I stood by to hear the deputy was okay. Bill didn't hear and went into the room thinking I was behind him. He soon realized I wasn't.

I don't recall just what all was said, the speaker was upset that they were losing the ranch. Upset that Bhagwan had been forced off and some general statements of other complaints. They did not apologize for any of the crimes or other activities they participated in.

The following week, at the appointed time, I stood on the courthouse steps and sold the property back to the mortgage lender. To be sure there would be no questions about the sale, I made sure that I read every part of the ranch's boundaries on the deed. It was a long sale. The boundaries of such a large ranch weren't like property in town. They were not as straight and well defined. They veered back and forth as the property bumped up against other property and BLM land.

But the story doesn't end there.

After a couple years of trying to find a buyer, the mortgage company sold it to a man named Dennis Washington in the 1990s. He was a wealthy industrialist from Montana.

The local paper posted the sales report. Not sure just how it started but four of us, The Dalles Fire Chief, our Personnel Director, our Communications Director and I decided to go down the day he took possession. We arrived mid-morning and made contact with some employees of Washington. Because this was private property, we could not just walk in and take a self-guided tour. I asked if they minded if we looked around. They said go ahead.

They weren't sure why their boss bought the ranch. He had purchased another cult's property in Montana a few years before. Their response to us asking was, "I guess he just likes buying cult property."

None of us had thought to bring along a camera, but it is still, a good 20-25 years later, pretty clear in my mind.

First, we explored the "Jesus Grove" housing where Sheela and her closest captains resided. This was modular housing. Several units had been put together, in a hub, to form the group.

Most of the rooms were empty, but Sheila's round bed was still there. I imagined that she planned her nefarious schemes sitting in that space. The reason they left it behind remained unclear. I remember thinking that it was one item no one wanted anything to do with. The followers wouldn't touch it even to destroy it.

She had an escape tunnel into a small ditch. The passage was about ten to fifteen feet long, as I recall, and about 4 feet in diameter. Corrugated drainage pipe lined the edges. The bottom had a floor about two feet wide made of wood with a rug covering it. The two directors couldn't wait to check it out. One of the things I liked about our county Personnel Director was his enthusiasm for life. He was like a kid exploring things for the first time. I let them get about halfway when I told them to look at the rug. You never know how many bodies were pulled through there.

They stopped and looked back at my smiling face, and continued. As they got close to the outside covering, I reminded them they should be watching out for rattlesnakes. That drew a tad bit more concern, but like curious cats they had to go on. They opened up the end door covering to see the ditch it led into on the other side. No snakes.

We continued our self-guided tour and went into the Bhagwan's complex. It was empty. His housing, again modular units, included a stainless steel emergency room where the doctor could take care of almost any problem. He had a large swimming pool in a section. Several garages once housed his Rolls Royces. Other than that there wasn't much left. People stripped everything of value long before our arrival.

The complex, ten acres +/-, was enclosed by a deer proof fence eight to ten feet high. The grounds around the garages were graveled. There was a lot of open space between the compound and most of the fencing.

We went over to the large "greenhouse" turned meeting arena. The south doors were open, and we went inside. It was a massive building. The stage where Bhagwan gave his lectures sat in the middle of the east wall. Dominating the building, taking up a full wall at the north end was that beautiful view of the rock formations and river.

The landscape through that well-placed window was beautiful. Natural rugged stone columns framed a glimpse of the John Day River. As we walked around inside, the Fire Chief noted that their sprinkler system was up to code. All the better for Washington.

The grounds of the property had returned to the native grass and weeds over time. We drove north on the road and saw where the Rajneesh had grown grapes and built a medium sized barn. There was fencing up, but it was wooden, not the usual barbed wire. The Rajneesh sold cattle to a company in England that prized their hides. The hide's lack of scratches from barbed wire made it desirable to English markets. Their time in India helped them make these connections.

I hadn't realized that those scratches from cows rubbing against the wire caused scars, which remained and were visible in the hides. Since the Rajneesh didn't use barbed wire, the coat was free from any injuries. The result presented a better-looking product.

We then drove through the downtown area. Everything was closed up and empty. The bookstore, where there used to be a few articles of clothing sold and lots of books and paraphernalia with Bhagwan's picture on everything, was now empty with some overturned furnishings. Driving on through the "city" and into the back area, everything turned back to the native grass.

We then decided to visit the funeral pyre. We located the road and followed it to the site. This was the same location that they used to cremate the Japanese drowning victim. The one that gave them the fireworks display on July 4th, 1985 that the Antelope Peace officers thought funny. And who knows how many others, if any. No proof, just suspicions.

The setting was beautiful. Encased in a "grove" of the rock formations prevalent in the area, was the funeral pyre and a large grassy hill with a gentle slope. It was ideal for the people to sit and partake of the spectacle of the funeral pyre. The rock formations towered over the scene by over a hundred feet.

The funeral pyre was enclosed in a Plexiglas wall several feet high. There was a small entrance on the southwest side. Over the fire, maybe 2' X 3' above the pyre, was a chimney. It was wide at the bottom and narrowed down to just a foot or two at the top, a good 20'-30' feet tall.

It was made of a brown metal, matching the color of the rocks with a lighter brown metal holding the corners together. It was a good match for the surrounding area.

The pyre itself was about 2' high X 10' long X 6' wide. It was made of cinder block and a massive meshed metal screen over the top; it reminded me of a large barbecue pit. Inside were tubes and gas jets. There was a walkway around the base of the hole made of concrete. The Plexiglas wall was about three feet away from the pit on all sides.

To the east of the pit was a bunker with eye slits at the height of the pyre.

We went around to see what the insides looked like. It was the control room, of course. There the slits were at eye level, about 5 to 6 feet from the ground. There were a few dials and knobs on the wall facing the pyre. The one dial showed a temperature range of up to 2500 degrees.

The Fire Chief said that would be about right for an outside pyre. The fuel for the fire was propane, although all tanks had been removed.

On the rock formations were small ledges. I have been told that the Rajneesh sat on the grassy hill and on these shelves singing, dancing and performing other actions as bodies were cremated.

As I stood there, I imagined a painting I once saw that showed the fires of hell and rock formations, very much like these, where demons danced with grinning evil grins as the souls were thrown into the fire.

We left, had lunch in Shaniko, and headed on home. The one thing that astonished me was there had been no vandalism. Buildings and grounds were starting to deteriorate, but no one had come down and tried to enact vengeance on the property. The locals were glad to see the Rajneesh gone, but weren't interested in committing any criminal actions.

There would be more occasions that I visited the camp. The Dalles Chamber of Commerce sponsored a leadership class for area business people. The Chamber Director had lived in Maupin for a lot of her life. Her father was in charge of two local mills in Maupin and Tygh Valley.

Part of her curriculum was to expose the business people of The Dalles to the other areas of Wasco County. The field trip through some of these smaller communities in the county included a visit to the Ranch. I played tour guide for several of these trips.

When we started out either the Director or I would ask how many people had been to Dufur. Dufur was a town about 16 miles south of The Dalles. Of the thirty people or so who took the class only a few raised their hands. When asked how many had gone farther south there were only one or two hands raised. Hence the trip.

The Director wanted them to see there was more to Wasco County than The Dalles and reminded them that they had customers that came up from these areas to conduct business here.

I was surprised that so many had never gone further before attending these trips. Of course, I had been there several times, including being a supervisor in the boys' dorm and clerking, among other things, at the County Fair in Tygh Valley. I enjoyed this area, and its people, long before I decided to run for sheriff.

If I had given it some thought, though, I would have realized that Wasco County wasn't much different than other places. The people in the larger communities often don't get out and around to the rural areas. They focus on their life in the city and forget there is more country out there. Our people didn't forget completely. They erected an antelope statue that sits in front of the county courthouse in The Dalles in honor of the resilient people of the town of Antelope.

I have always admired the fortitude and strength of those that live off the land. They work hard. They get their hands dirty. They speak their minds and for the most part, they are real people with no phoniness. They contribute to the community and endure when many other businessmen would close shop.

CHAPTER 18

Time passed. At first, Washington tried to give the ranch to the State of Oregon. They refused to accept it. It would cost too much money to renovate and keep up. The people living close to the ranch were skeptical and concerned. They didn't know what he planned to do, and some were afraid he would sell it to another cult.

While he was making a decision as to what to do, he had a caretaker live in the farmhouse with his family. The young man was from a local ranching family. He did the best he could to keep things in order. Then the fire came and everything changed.

I don't recall just what year it occurred, but a wildfire swept through the South County. The fire destroyed tens of thousands of acres. It passed through the ranch area, burning the Rajneesh compound and beyond. The bulk of the buildings remained untouched. There was only minor damage to some of the outposts.

Washington donated the camp to a Christian Organization called Young Life. They are a Seattle based non-profit company with camps all over the northwest. At the time, they had a thriving camp on the coast. Some children remained outside of their ability to reach due to distance. It was too hard to bus kids from places like Bend and The Dalles. A camp in the eastern part of the state appealed to their growing needs, so they took Washington up on his offer.

Young Life is an outreach for young people in the large cities. They provide camp experiences for different organizations, along with their own missional outreach events. When they took over, the county allowed them to use the facilities but restricted occupancy to a little over 1000 people at any given time. This has yet to be a problem, given that most of the workers were temporary volunteer help. Some come for a year, others for a few weeks and others arrive with their kid's group to help with preparing food, etc. This type of labor keeps the cost down and allows for more kids to come to camp. A handful of individuals have taken root and live in their RVs. These do volunteer work year round.

Washington has donated millions of dollars to the rebuilding and upkeep. It was named in his honor. While the purpose remains to serve its own needs during the summer, it also opens the property up to other organizations. It goes about its business with no adverse impact on the surrounding communities.

My last trip to the ranch was the summer of 2010. During the summer, many churches in our community send their youth to another area to help missionaries for a short time. Someone came up with the idea that The Dalles should be treated as a mission field. Several youth groups from area churches came together to be "missionaries." They worked in the community, helped build a few things, and ran a local VBS.

Since their focus was on missions, they stayed the night out in tents. One of the ranchers, who was a local physician, opened up his grounds for housing, restrooms, shower areas, food areas, etc. The kids worked in the community then came back to the ranch at night to bond.

The first week included a history lesson of the area. I was asked to come in one of those evenings and give a "15" minute talk on the Rajneesh. It turned into about an hour or so discourse with questions and answers.

Bright and early the next morning I met with the group. We went on a pre-arranged tour of the ranch. The kids were still eating when I got there. They were running a tad late.

Just before we got into the two vans taking us down, I told them to think about how long it was going to take to get there. To consider the time on the county roads that were just gravel. And other important aspects of "rural" living.

We left Antelope and a couple of miles further we turned onto the county road leading south. The first thing I noticed was that many of the signs and posts the Rajneesh had erected were gone. I could still remember where they had been, but shadows were all that remained. To a person coming into the ranch proper now, the only sign of the Rajneesh occupation was the two doves on the dam. We came to the narrow county road leading down to the ranch. Much to my surprise, it had been paved by the Center.

We met up with our tour guide. I helped him fill some holes in the history of the ranch and gave him some more information as to what occurred. He told us they don't talk much about the Rajneesh when they give tours, preferring to focus on what the ranch stands for now.

The downtown mall area has been turned into dormitories. There is an area for those that remain for a short time, and some set aside for those that come for a year. There are also quarters for those that are married.

Most of the activity takes place in the area that used to be Jesus Grove, the hotel, and the "greenhouse." They have a large cafeteria where food is served family style. In that building, there is also a large laundry room. Volunteers from the groups that come down do the bulk of the work preparing meals, serving, and doing laundry for their groups. They are supervised by camp staff.

The hotel has been turned into a dormitory for the groups coming in. The leaders of those groups are responsible for their charges. They moved the visitor's center from the south part of the "city," which was across from the Fire Hall, to the activity compound and use it as an intake center for the kids to check in.

The "greenhouse" has been turned into an indoor activity center. The floor is now wood, and several basketball courts, as well as an indoor skate park, are set up. There was still quite a bit of room left that hadn't been designated yet and was being used for storage when we were down there. My son, a local youth pastor at the time, told me they put in a rock climbing wall. The Young Life people have done a fantastic job of turning the ranch into a retreat for children. I never thought that a place that caused so much pain could be transformed into a haven for grace. It goes to show that it's not the place but the people that shape the future.

WORDS FROM THE AUTHOR

Why Now?

t was time. I had been intending to write for quite some time and had written a few lines, but hadn't put them together and hadn't covered all the things that happened on my watch. Many have asked me to give a written account of what Wasco County endured during the Rajneesh's time in the county and how it impacted the citizens. Which brings me to the final reason: Sharia law.

Some politicians even suggested that the Rajneesh be allowed to form their own county that would be "ruled" by them. They were trying to see if they could bring "peace" to the region, but it would have been a capitulation to their demands instead of those of our Constitution. They would have no oversight by anyone.

One of the things that allowed the Rajneesh to get by with so much was the fear of insulting their religion. Many people backed away from holding them accountable to the laws of the land in dread of being labeled racists. We were fortunate in our county. Though we did not have a large population, we did have enough voters to keep the Rajneesh from coming into power and ruling illegally, as they did Antelope. We have several counties in Oregon that are large in square miles, but small in population. Three of those counties adjoin Wasco County, and none of them had over 2000 people. If the Rajneesh had settled into one of them, they could have overcome county government, elected their own people to all the elected positions, and made mayhem of our laws.

The Rajneesh insisted that they be given special treatment and used their religion against anyone that opposed them. They were not interested in obeying legislation to get their way. They committed many crimes in the process. We need to realize that our laws are in place for a reason. People cannot come into our communities and demand that their "laws" should take precedent over those tested over time that align with the Constitution and Bill of Rights. Many of the laws they wish to institute are not compatible. It should not be allowed period.

People need to stand against those that would abuse American laws and use their "religion" as a basis to cry discrimination.

A group bent on getting their way, no matter what can wreak havoc in a small community. Enforcing the laws broken by the Rajneesh cost Wasco County hundreds of thousands of dollars that could have been used in better ways. There was the additional charge of tens of thousands of hours of employees' time spent trying to defend the county and the citizens. Those costs were difficult to calculate. And that doesn't even cover the emotional cost to all involved.

We are seeing the demands of Muslims starting to impact the ability of communities to enforce laws. They have a right to be in our country legally. They have a right to live and work here. They have a right to worship as they see fit. They do not have the right to intimidate the local population to get their way and have their Sharia laws supplant those that have been in existence in our country for years. Our hard earned freedoms are not compatible.

When people from a different country come to America, the expectation is they will obey the laws. No group, of any kind, should be allowed to undermine the judicial system. The Rajneesh tried. It was an expensive lesson. We should learn from that historical fact.

Made in the USA
Monee, IL
18 January 2020